first here and then far

first here and then far

SELECTED POEMS 1971–2024

david zieroth

HARBOUR
PUBLISHING

HARBOUR PUBLISHING CO. LTD.
P.O. Box 219, Madeira Park, BC, VON 2HO
www.harbourpublishing.com

COVER ILLUSTRATION by Daniel Koppersmith
EDITED by Peter Midgley
COVER AND TEXT DESIGN by Libris Simas Ferraz / Onça Publishing
PRINTED AND BOUND in Canada
PRINTED on 100% recycled + FSC® certified paper

HARBOUR PUBLISHING acknowledges the support of the Canada Council for the Arts, the Government of Canada, and the Province of British Columbia through the BC Arts Council.

CATALOGUING DATA AVAILABLE FROM LIBRARY AND ARCHIVES CANADA
Title: First here and then far : selected poems 1971-2024 / David Zieroth.
Names: Zieroth, David, author.
Identifiers: Canadiana (print) 20240413032 | Canadiana (ebook)
     2024041621X | ISBN 9781990776915 (softcover) | ISBN 9781990776922
     (EPUB)
Subjects: LCGFT: Poetry.
Classification: LCC PS8599.I47 F57 2024 | DDC c811/.54—dc23

For Marlow, Lucian, Robin, Liam, Evan,
Marjalena, Simon, Laura, John, Margery

CONTENTS

THE HUNTERS OF THE DEER

The ten men will dress in white
to match the snow and leave the last
farmhouse and the last woman, going
north into the country of the deer. It
is from there, and from past there, that
the wind begins that can shake
every window in the house and leaves
the woman wishing she had moved away
five years and five children ago.

During the day the father of her children
will kill from a distance. With the others
he will track and drive each bush
and at least once he will kill before
they stop and come together for
coffee in scratched quart jars. And
sometimes the November sun will glint
on the rifles propped together in the snow.

In the evening, as they skin and gut,
they talk about the one that ran three
miles on a broken leg and the bitch wolf
they should have shot and how John
the bachelor likes eating more than
hunting and they pass the whisky
around to keep warm. In the house
the woman makes a meal from pork.

These men are hunters and later,
standing in bright electrically lighted
rooms they are embarrassed by the
blood on their clothes and although the
woman nods and seems to understand,
she grows restless with their talk.
She has not heard another woman in fourteen days.

And when they leave, the man sleeps
and his children sleep while the woman
waits and listens for the howling of
wolves. To the north, the grey
she-wolf smells the red snow and howls.
Tonight, while other hunters sleep, she
drinks at the throat.

GLENELLA, MANITOBA

The village, east of highway five,
huddles by the only railway tracks in
fifty miles. One white grain elevator
tells you where you are, from any
direction. After four fires the place
is still big enough to have the
usual buildings: school, hall,
station, hotel and two stores.
Sunday evenings, a passenger
train; Thursday, a freight.
There are no factories here
and no luxuries. On two sides
there are hay fields and country;
machinery and men sometimes move
there. North of here is nothing.

On Saturday night there are locals
sick in the pub and Crazy John sitting
in the poolhall where he's sat for years
watching the spinning balls, the young men,
who knows what. Visitors soon discover
there are some here who like
what they have lived through. Mostly, there
are young men who stand waiting
with their hands made fists in
pockets that are empty, young men
who know that Winnipeg
(200 miles south and not big enough
for a place on the map of the world
in the post office), that Winnipeg
is where the world begins.

1) 120 MILES NORTH OF WINNIPEG

My grandfather came here years ago,
family of eight. In the village,
nine miles away, they knew him as
the German and they were suspicious, being
already settled. Later he was
somewhat liked, still later
forgotten. In winter everything
went white as buffalo bones and
the underwear froze on the line
like corpses. Often the youngest
was sick. Still he never thought
of leaving. Spring was always greener
than he'd known and summer had
kid-high grass with sunsets big
as God. The wheat was thick,
the log house chinked and warm.
The little English he spoke
he learned from the thin grey lady
in the one-room school, an hour away
by foot. The oldest could hunt, the youngest
could read. They knew nothing of
the world he'd left, and forgotten,
until 1914 made him an alien and
he left them on the land he'd come to,
120 miles north of Winnipeg.

2) DETENTION CAMP, BRANDON, MANITOBA

On the morning of the fourth day,
two men were missing. Later, brought
back, they talked for a while
of some part of summer they'd seen,
then they were quiet, turned bitter,
even a little crazed: these received
no letters from the outside and spoke now
of nothing they wished to return to.
Bodies at night would moan, asleep
with others somewhere who dreamt
of them. The sunrise on the wall
became a condition, the sunset a way
of counting days. The prisoners carried
these things close to their bodies.
This my grandfather came to know
before leaving.

He did not celebrate his homecoming.
His wife was older, his children
came to him less. Even the sky
was not as blue as he'd remembered,
and the harvest, three-quarters done,
reminded him too often of wasted
time, of war in Europe. Winter
came too quickly that year and
next spring the turning of the earth
held no new surprises.

FATHER

Twice he took me in his hands and shook
me like a sheaf of wheat, the way a dog shakes
a snake, as if he meant to knock out my tongue
and grind it under his heel right there
on the kitchen floor. I never remembered
what he said or the warnings he gave; she
always told me afterwards, when he
had left and I had stopped my crying. I
was eleven that year and for seven more years
I watched his friends laughing and him
with his great hands rising and falling
with every laugh, smashing down on his knees
and making the noise of a tree when it cracks
in winter. Together they drank chokecherry
wine and talked of the dead friends and the
old times when they were young, and because
I never thought of getting old, their
youth was the first I knew of dying.

Sunday before church he would trim
his fingernails with the hunting knife
his East German cousins had sent, the same
knife he used for castrating pigs and
skinning deer: things that had nothing
to do with Sunday. Communion once
a month, a shave every third day, a
good chew of snuff, these were the things
that helped a man to stand in the sun for
eight hours a day, to sweat through each
cold hailstorm without a word, to freeze
fingers and feet to cut wood in winter, to do
the work that bent his back a little more
each day down toward the ground.

Last Christmas, for the first time, he
gave presents, unwrapped and bought
with pension money. He drinks mostly coffee
now, sleeping late and shaving every day.
Even the hands have changed: white, soft,
unused hands. Still he seems content
to be this old, to be sleeping in the middle
of the afternoon with his mouth open as if there
is no further need for secrets, as if he is
no longer afraid to call his children fools
for finding different answers, different lives.

THE MOUNTAINS HAVE NOT YET ENTERED

The mountains have not yet entered
my dreams and become familiar as the cities
and the old places where the land
is flat and the shadows are my own.
The mountains will come, their high grey
iguana fringe of peaks will come
broken and shoved up into the snow and ice.
They will come as the violent cities
came, as the flat land came and went.

There will be no struggle with these
mountains. It is best to go as high as
the loggers' road, above the valley
where the air is cold and thin forever.
If this place does not warm and feed you it will
warm and feed no others. You will find
other ways to survive. Those who come after you
riding in from the world will find only
your campfires, left from the time
when only fire made you warm.

The daylight blue of these mountains
will heal you, the white of their snow
will mark each day a new beginning.
You will recognize as yours the land as high
as the timberline, the golden tamaracks
and the soft green pines that wrap around
the shoulders of the mountain. And above that,
that is your land too, above everything
in the fusion of rock with rock.
Your boundaries start at the river
and end in the yellow sun, hanging there,
where you reach it from the snow.

It is a safe place to live. At first
the dark will make you cry out, you will be
eager for faces. That will pass.
Eventually the night air will surround you
like the breath of God. When the end comes
you will not be thinking of it.
The river will carry your bones out of the valley
down to the people and the houses of light.
They will be used as driftwood—that is
as it should be: you cannot live here
if you do not change.

It will be years before they discover the space
you lived in. They will come after you
with their equipment and their maps.
They will trace back and find
the trails of other men, and above that
they will find your place, the
strange markings and the hollow rocks.
They will spend the winter here but they
will not survive. Only the child will stay.
He alone has seen your flesh bind together
the mountains as easily as ice. In time
he will enter your world. Then there will be
two of you. The mountains will enter
a long and pleasant spring.

BEAUTIFUL WOMAN

1.

Beautiful woman, you crown the hours
and we grow wonderful, we grow secret
in the assumption of our life. How easily
the electric night warms us. Fish
swim past the edges of our bed, oceans
in their mouths. The morning will never come
and break down this fever to be mad in each other's
warm white skin. We go down
like children, we go down into a great moaning
with silence forgotten and floating through the ceiling
like balloons. See me, see me dancing
to your terrible music, woman. The room
is filling with candles, the sun
is inches away: it smells
of your hair and lies writhing in your palm.
See again the sun and the bed wet with warm rain.
Wave after wave it comes, wave
after wave stones
break open at our touch, small bones break free and drift
out of you into me. And the skin
becomes water and salt shuddering
out past fingers—blood-filled and animal—
toward the centre
of a thick and velvet earth where the sun
burns a hole in the sky.

2.

Yet even from this bed
the anger rises day by day
and digs trenches to fortify its seed. So we
swear, accuse, sometimes punch flat-handed
the stubborn skin. You tell me
what it means to wait and work afternoons
with dishes and floors. You tell me
my friends who pace and strut ignore you, or notice
only your sex. How you hate them!
See your tears fly out at them like diamond-headed
spikes. See that it's me you've hit.
Let that sound surround our bed, let it
fill up the room as high as the windows.
Put your hungriest cats to prowl inside my skin.
Let nothing escape: the mouth
will stretch and harden into my best smile.
(You know this is not like a movie, you know
this is not in our dream—yet it continues.)
Everywhere muscles are dying. Out of my throat
you will hear me cursing, you will hear me
roaring. When it is my turn
nothing will change. The mirror
will fall, history will vomit at your name.

3.

It is morning and the yellow sun falls
through the window like a stone. In the kitchen
the dishes wait and bits of swollen meat
have stuck to the sides of knives. All around us
broken flesh is aching. Tonight
we will go deep into our powerful
bodies again. Or we will do nothing
and survive just the same. Woman,
wake up and hold me, I have
nowhere else to take my anger. Wake up and let
your hands spread like warmth along my back.
Now that the skin is dead. Now
that both the music and the bruises have gone.
And all that remains refuses to begin
without falling, is
caught and held in the light that spills
off the floor and stains the bed
like wine.

LAKE

In the morning, along the vacant shore,
when the water is still cool
and the trees bend down as if to drink,
there is a quietness like the deer who come for water
in the small round seconds of the dawn: the denials
are forgotten, the tough work of balance and
maintenance and hope has not yet begun.
It is a different place now, this view
that is a panorama, that is also
a reflection, these million leaves
opening like mouths to the sun and to the light
that rolls down the mountain, down
to the water in the urgent greeting that
turns the water blue and white and once more
familiar like the beautiful
brown hands of summer.

By evening, even the water does not flow
toward me: there is no order
outside the kind I need to impose and I
step back so easily into
a void at the end of the day where the
calm is waiting and I can
kneel down and let it touch my hands, let it
cool the palms and wash upwards over the shoulders
and the thin blind eyes. Now the lake
is company enough. Later I may turn,
leave the great dark face of the water
and take those first sweet steps
back to earth.

WAITING AT EVENING

The sun almost down and the day
settling inside me like sediment, its
terrible movements keep stirring while
in front of me the mountains go
purple, go bright in the sun, the snow
shining like a light. And the evening
in slow and constant change now that I am alone
and waiting for the nighthawks to come, alone
with the robins in the green grass,
the casual movements of horses beyond the fence
where the apple blossoms are falling
like snow or light, the crystal
evening light. And everywhere the day shifts
inside me with its own kind of life and my need
to separate it out, to give it
a sense of its own so it can
leave me.

And still I will inhabit
the bitter geography of my own making, a place
where the roots rise up
and choke me or hold too tightly
when I want most of all to move. And the small
dry bones of friendship, they are here too,
the repeat performances of my failures when I have
stepped out of my heart and out of
my friends' lives in order to survive.
And for them there is still
the greatest need to hurt
again and again
                            and still be loved.
Or at least be held as the light holds me now
folding and bending around me so softly

that for a moment I lose sight of it and know
only the sharp brooding hazards of the day:
it is always this way, what I change
I also destroy. Now I build from
new dreams and some dreams I can't tell anyone.

          And still the dark rises,
coming up like an army of the blind, bending
before my vision like glass. And there, a
jet, moving out of the east like a
carefully drawn chalk line, becoming itself
a cloud. It becomes time to go inside
again, there are still
no clues. The nighthawks
have not yet arrived. There are only a few stars.

BAPTISM

In mid-river we join the ancient force
of mud and leaves moving in their journey
down the face of the continent and after
the first dance of leaving
one element for another, we fall quiet,
waiting for the silence to give us a
glimpse of history. In mid-river, it is
still possible to imagine Thompson's world,
without roads or bridges, rivers that
go back beyond white lives into the rocks
that push and fold, fault and break
as the new world rises from
the old.
          Yet this is still our river.
It does not matter that we are not
the first, what we will find today
has been found a hundred times before: it is
the story of men meeting water,
as if there were a time, or faith,
when all of us were rivers, one
strength sliding out of the sky and into
the sea, one direction in us all.

But the river churns here and beats along the shore.
It picks up speed on the outside curve
cutting past the cottonwoods and under the deadfalls
that sweep across the water like the last arm of the land
and the water takes command.
I bend my paddle in my hand and my friend
digs in but there are branches like dead fingers in our faces
and there can be
no avoidance now, water comes up and the
snag bends us down until my lungs

are in the water, they are stones and I am
grabbing for the tree as if it were
my friend while the current sucks on me and my arms
go heavy as lead, a scream
goes dead in my throat, we do not
belong here, it bubbles and swallows
silt, the taste of ice,
there are blue stars somewhere and all the sounds of water
are alive and they pour in my ears,
into my eyes as if the river is already sure
how deep it will carry me,
what it will do with my skin, how it will dissolve
and burst and thin out the blood and I roll over
in a dream of clouds, willows, catch the edge
of a bank beaver's hole, brown mud like gold on my palm,
my feet still pulling for the ocean and then they find
gravel, the river rock, the river
pushes me away and I am shaking in the air again,
shaking for my friend riding the canoe's bottom
like a drunken pea pod, he grinds on the bank
a hundred yards downstream, his boots sucked off,
his body like a hole in the sand.

I breathe in the sun, take it yellow
into the body that spits grey in the river.
The baptism is over.
We have walked away without the grace of
fish or grebes, and the river is still the same.
I sit and watch the water with the oldest eyes of men:
if I trust the river, I will be
caught in it, rolled backwards into the
simplest race of all, the first, and the river is hard, it is
carnal and twists like an animal going blind in the rain,

but it leaves me pouring water from my shoe and then I see
him stand, wave, we have
first words.
Soon our paddles will bite the water but they will not
break it: our place on earth is rich enough,
the sudden rush of birdsong, our own
mid-river laughter as the warmth begins again.

THE TRUCK THAT COMMITTED SUICIDE

In one major operation he tore out her
big black heart of an engine and threw in another.
His fingers worked over her,
tightening and touching and leaving
little drops of blood that mixed with the oil and the mud.
He drove her on pavement and gravel and dirt,
on ice and muck and trails that ended like lines in the dust.
He drove her on the road to work,
down the Mile Hill where the deer
came out of the mountains on the way to the river, for that is
their work, to get across the road, their daily task
looking both ways and taking their chances when the
big trucks come down on them, the loggers and the
cowboys, the tourists and the housewives up early,
the drunks trying hard in the middle of the night
with the booze inside them like a golden plastic fruit,
seeing a pair of golden eyes and sliding
into them, opening them up in the middle of the highway
that is a slab of noise and light, the wind
whips back and forth through their big mule ears, the hair
ruffles and they look like they're asleep,
can't quite get up yet. And later there is a stain
on the asphalt like old red paint where the ravens hop
forward and peer into the eyes as if to ask
one last question, and over near the edge there are
other birds taking their
share of the work as
his truck goes by.

Rolling down the hill into work
and the sight of the ravens black as old women started
touching off nerves that went down deep, bringing back
a wave that went through the man and then
over him, a direct hit, leaning forward into something
not quite known and the truck felt it.
The two of them at once
crossed the yellow line, crossed the asphalt on the
other side and touched the guard rail.
There was a humping sound like the sigh of
extinction, a wrenching as the things that fit together
broke apart, doors swung open and she tipped and broke and
roared. His head
touched the windshield that broke then
shattered into all the smallest pieces,
some falling out and down to the ground
even before the two of them stopped at the bottom of
the Mile Hill, rolled up
against a tree with their black wheels spinning slowly, a tree
on fire now and burning with them and
adding its odd woody smell to their
oily exploding he / she smell, the smell
that would still cling and hold them together
after the necessary tasks of removal and identification,
after the separation and the final washing
there would still be that one vague and bodiless smell
it would stay the way it had formed in the last moment
out of paint and sweat and dust and blood,
one smell   so strong and rich and different it left other men sad
and gagging under nearby trees
retching and hawking and then recognizing once again
the sound of the ravens arriving for work
the smell in their hairless wings.

OUT WALKING

Sometimes I go out for walks
walks along the edge of the earth,
on goat paths along limestone sides of mountains, walks
on game trails that lead back into
the high tipped-up corners of valleys, and I scare up
a wolverine running low to the ground like a devil badger
flinging back its head in the dark outline of
fang and tongue and fang. And I
stop at the edge of the creek
where the water is warm among the marks of things
that are webbed and hooved and clawed.

Sometimes I walk in the rain
when the great storms build.
They are born in all the inhuman places
and cannot be seen coming off their dark oceans.
The thunder breaks its back across our roofs
and the rain turns all its dark eyes on us.
A drop at a time, it wedges out
the holy artifacts; our fathers' graves
slide into the sea. The cool green
world surrounds us, makes its move to life
while we stand still, losing ground to the rain,
watching the mushrooms
that come thrusting up between us.
    Once I fell on my knees before it all,
on my knees in the mud with the million tapping drops
sounding on my skull like all the drums
of Africa. I watched the clouds grind down the mountains.
I saw birds impale themselves like soldiers
on the high white lightning rods of men.
Everywhere the rain was sending me
a message: you are fed, you are

rain, your cities are dust,
you are here to witness the fertile place opening,
the dark warm places growing darker, deeper,
taking in the sound and the smell and the dumb life again.

Now the land slopes down
into mushrooms, moss, dark needles.
I go deep in a cave, smell the rain running through the land
but here the clay soil floats up through my hair and the light
goes down to the bottom, all the way back where it rests
on a white and weightless bone
and this I will carry home,
under my coat like a treasure, safe, dry.
There is a place above my fire for
the bones of the old lives when all the liquids have left
and the dust settles slowly
while I sit here and imagine blurred things on the mountain
grey shapes rising like pines
something wild running for the water, sinking down on its
knees at the river and turning to meet
wolves, dogs or men.

Outside the rain slants down as if someone has thrown it,
it pulls the leaves to the sky like banners.
The clouds dissolve and set free the sun
where it rolls in a blue-bonnet sky. And I think
the earth is the place to begin,
the ground around a door,
the meadow turning slowly into
forest: this is the first mystery
if only because it is not human and will not stop
the moment our own selves are rich enough
to do without

the earth around us: the great movements
of the soil will continue, the leaves
that turn the black and white of soil and sun
to green, the lake that is
rain that is lake again.
The tree flings off its seeds without compassion,
the wood gives up its sunshine in the flame
and none of us were asked
what part we want to play. Our place
is the mind that sees the death of foxes,
birds, the weak and small
and goes beyond the pain, looks
beyond the mountain and into the mountain range.
We have the power that gives the bird
its name and raises us to
the gods we once fashioned out of
bones. Out of the leaves and out of the earth
that made the bones, out of the earth
where all the bones will end.

JOURNEY: GOING IN / GETTING OUT

Getting beyond the ragged perimeters and
ugly edges thrown up by the clutter in myself,
going inside and getting past the grit stacked like factories
in my blood, then creeping into fields,
I want to go step by step
in that direction, into the full bloom of earth.

There I can open to a centre that is
choked by the staleness of daily bread,
I can run parallel to words, at last
like starting up a mountain: getting above the forest
and then past the warm rocky nest of the marmots,
becoming small beneath the sky,
rising up somehow
like wind, like the air inside the wind
where all energies combine
and re-combine and are eliminated—

and sometimes finding there
only dreams, brains, calypso battles in the Friday night,
lust like the swing of a baseball bat or the guts of
an army feasting outside the gate,
flesh-headed soldiers dancing in the night—
sometimes finding there one who is already
waiting, standing up like a bear,
shivering at its first sight of me,
its face like a bull's-eye of blood.

Whether there is peace or war or truce,
whether I find good or nothing good,
still the body remains,
legs that have learned years ago
how to carry the sickening heart, how to
drag it down to the curve in the river
or to the quickening edge of the crevasse.
Body, wise like an animal,
hunted and chased through the tangle,
driven at times to the ground
but breaking through into the open,
always carrying its rider back to the sun and the fire.
Step by step, this stranger
pulls me back to the deep caves of rest,
then pulls me out by the navel
until I am plugged into the peaceful bright
shock of the outer world—it penetrates
like a shaft from an early sun,
white arrow glancing off a mountain and going
far beneath the edges of the skin.

WHEN MY COWS BREAK LOOSE

There are cows in the library again
brown shaggy natural shapes
crowding the ladies in search of romance
and I can smell
the wet sides that have to be dealt with
just before milking
I sometimes see cows in clouds.
My daughter knows little about cows
(and she knows that from books),
she is more like her mother than me
I am more like the cows
that come hulking out of the past and want to be
pressed into place, like the books
row on row, or in the stores, mooing softly under Muzak,
bawling at the edge of the fence, hurting
in their bags when I stayed late
at a baseball game, in a neighbour's field
Or else they're wanting their calves
again, bawling in their big hearts
cut off from
offspring
and I want to take the willow switch now
stop the milk stool descending on Rosie's back
and all the stones
and the dog makes them run until their bags
fly out this way and back,
milk and meat and his eager breeding
and maybe once a summer
a wind in the farthest corner
scatters all the flies and stops the itching warbles
a cool sun
the broken fence leading to alfalfa beyond where I'm
straining to read
a bell   tinkling through the heat

1956: THE AMBITION OF THE ELDEST SON

Running the horses,
my shirt flicking behind me like wings
when the land made room for me—

I did not see my ambition then,
how it turned my head to peer down the road:
I dreamt car instead of animal

and trusted none of the women
home-grown by the same tall teachers
(it would have been like marrying

my sister. I needed distant flesh, not
the mouths that held old words
about me) and walking down the lane

nothing reached out to hold:
I saw green drown or burn or
knocked to the ground, as the dead are

laid out, punctured and dry.
I embraced the road instead, my father's
not-speaking as if he knows

we must ride as the mother says
into the cities, into the houses
keep wordless between the white lines

steadying the self as we pound home
toward the bright children sprawled before
gadgets in the rec room I am building

under the ground, out of love, I stay
ahead of longing: which is a wasted field
nothing to plough under

a narrow field where hot animals
must stand day after day
waiting for the gate to come open.

1956: THE OLD LUTHERAN PASTOR

I say *God is love* and they
rise in their pews
and sing: around me
they are at last united, humble
before the Host, and every Sunday I can
fill the church built by their fathers
until they burst out again
gulping the deep air
lighting their smokes.
                    Wine is not wine,
bread is not bread:
I intone the mystery, prepare them
to meet their sins
the daily irritation with land
frozen too long, burning too long,
yielding envy by the bushel.
This drives them away
for they cannot let down their pride
to me, to God, to the neighbour who sits
red and stiff across the aisle.

Casting water on the babies, dropping
dirt into the graves, training the young ones
to be firm in their fathers' faith—those boys
who burn to be righteous, who swear by sunsets—
I join them all together. I am
their roof and old and always remembering now
those others who come only in need,
the pregnant and the quickly converted,
not the old women who have lived beyond their men
for they are Jerusalem to me.

The ones who walk past
as I stand at the door shaking hands
will not give me anything—
they compare God to His world and see
holiness is a pale thing, a hand fumbling
half-caught in black—they do not see
how I close the heavy door at last and look out
toward the graves with their bright willows
dancing: the dead come to befriend me again
and beyond us—look—the land shimmers.

WHEN THE STONES FLY UP

In a country I cannot yet abandon,
the stones fly up from their fields,
they hover in the sky, they break open.
Their speech is a propelled speech.
Hundreds of them rise from their tasks.

In this country I can't tell
if today some special announcement
might be read. Do we listen everywhere
the same, on all continents
are stones filling the afternoon sky?

The fields lie empty,
the sky looks dead. In between
I am listening, careful how I move.
Once—we can all remember this sound—
when it threatened to rain
and the first drops hit,
I stood up, my voice talking:

to keep the stones in their place
it would say any prayer
any lie—it would have sworn any oath
that worked.

RETURNING TO A TOWN

Approaching a prairie town
I pass by fields and look across their
cultivated space toward the beating trees.
Waving on their streets,
poplar and maple hide retirement homes;
I imagine old wives criss-cross
between houses, their husbands
prowl the yards outside.
Nearing sunset, the dust sends out
its bleeding millions
with the strength of land and sun.

Entering town, I find I am
again standing in the baseball field, on snowy
streets I feel cold eating up my legs.
At the rink, men sweat
and go faster, then undress
in the corner behind the stove, climbing
out of pads and into their underwear jokes.
I sit in the café throwing jacks.
At night the combination poolhall
barbershop attracts me into its hooded light
and women from the high school
smoke in their brothers' cars, waiting.

Driving this street
I might see a kid step out of church
crying, women in black clot around him:
his uncle crushed under a machine
in a field, on a deathbed of dirt.
Across the street, safe under trees,
another boy pulls his coat tight—
he has seen the bully's tears,
the wind burns on the bully's cheeks.
The street empties its mourning into
both of them. In town
I am ready to meet a black car.

I arrive safely at my mother's door
in my father's street the legs go slow.
Each man walks toward home, well-known
by the stones in his field,
by the care he gave horses,
trees, his granaries. Or by his kids and
their returning, their electrical gifts,
their moments at the edge of town: where
the sidewalk ends
the great trees lift—and here
they wait, shyly, as the wind turns
and comes on.

THE FIELD

the field yokes post to soil and up
to the measureless sky—each
creates the field and takes its breath
from sketches of claw and twig,
from the hawk in the moment it spies
mouse, the sound of
grasshopper breaking in the bill of the
kestrel, the emigrant bobolink
singing from the liquid green stalks
that dance and dance and promise no end to
summer—field is summer

field makes the man speak, gives him
only one word that must say
tomorrow and *work* and *sorrow* yet he will not
deny field no matter how much
it blows away—field teaches him how to deceive
for it is here tractor sinks
into the soft under-mud, here the horses
carve out hoof-holes
in a season of tracks cutting the field
which is always square

field still dreams of the aspen root,
it hears the animals
faltering under the trees
and it accepts the bones,
it receives the blood of the buffalo
that came and rubbed and thrashed
and gave up its skull—now
through the layers, it is pulled up,
a man looks up from his field
(a curve of bone in his hand): only wind

the field is breath inside him:
at times he cannot know what he feels
until he stands in his field—or when
he looks out the window, his children
swing their feet under the table, he sees
a noon light falling in the fields
that are green (and young)
they become white and waiting
and always they spread away under his glance
creating bushy edges
where others stretch (and dream) and measure

THE BOAT

1.

I go back to the boat, and then
nothing—across the ocean
no peasant in a sheepskin
smiles and offers his calloused hand,
no milkmaid teases. Yet
at the lip of a decision
somewhere in Prussia or Poland
where the borderland shifts
under their bed, two of them
talk across the continental night,
the promise of land tumbling out
with every word—and the fear
never quite laid to rest
by the kiss, the thrust, and always
the promise, his great promise
and her looking up into the unborn night,
Europe crowding around, dark as a cowshed.

I dig up old letters, written
in a wavering hand, all gothic
swirls and I imagine
this is the Atlantic in their veins,
the boat rocking under them, night after night
then pitching them up
on a cold green land—so I imagine
when I trace back to the boat
and find no sign of them
stepping off, all the talk
at an end, the tough job beginning,
holding the fear close enough
to smell it—after all that salt sharp
air, still the slightest whiff
of dung.

2.

He goes back to the boat
and the boat is not there, it has
set out again and
all around the world it is
picking up its people, the ragged
ones who can't decide
and in the last moment a man
appears suddenly under a tree
at the end of their street—and they flee
to the water, to the boat
churning up the sea, throwing
up its citizenship of foam and tears.
These hopefuls reach
into their bundles and pull out icons, crusts,
potions that grandmothers made,
the old women who couldn't come
or wouldn't make it
but who wave and were the end of history
in that place
forgoing the boat for the comfort
forgoing the promise for the familiar fire.
The boat gets away
just as the old walls fall
and two people are clinging to each other
and to the dream approaching,
unaware that the new shore changes
with each curled wave,
and sand is what they share
with the settlements.

3.

So you go back to the boat
—and there is no foothold,
no bloodlines swim ashore, no rat
leaps along the anchor line
—and what still lives in you
that awoke and looked west
out of the huts?—
the slow wash against the sand, a lap lap
lapping that says over and over
nothing of you crosses this chasm,
all of you springs up
from this plank, this board
ripped from the ship and planted
here, sprouting into a wave-green tree
out of which your father fell,
out of which your mother decided
it was time to come down to earth

—and they took you
from the water's edge, and sat you down
in the middle of the continent, dusty
and without knowledge, and on the days
of the heavy rain, when the leaves curled down,
they could not understand
they would not remember
the old voices you kept hearing
in the rain.

THE BIRDS STAY WITH HIM

Years later
they would still be with him, flying inside:
black crows covering one October sky, then gone
till March, he sees them
jabbing at the yellow stooks, like flags
tossed out of trees, or
dangling from a belt, ten cents a pair of legs

the waxwing whose nest
his hand slipped into, the mother-bird gone,
robins after rain listen at the garden floor,
and one oriole flies in and splashes
sun colours
into the catbird air, quick pigeons
flying back and forth to town

and once an owl
falling from the top of the barn, shot
through the heart, flapping, falling,
sending chickens quickly
into their nighttime coops

Cranes taller than cattle
attack the grain fields: he came
not to kill but to watch and when they flew up
squawking, he felt his bare feet
burning in the sand

and through February, all white
and dark, he watched the roadside for a
horned lark
　　　　first eater of snow
and looking up once, he saw
swamp robins in the silver trees: later they might
haunt him for an afternoon but now they are
delicately turning their heads, casually
moving toward spring

BORN IN EUROPE

My mother was
expecting death, the way she said
her own mother had died
and I thought of the place where
the farm animals all must go.
No one really cried
but me: she was born in Europe and died wanting
flowered dresses: they say
the doctors took away the tubes at last
but how?
I never asked and went outside
and took my heart and laid it in the snow.

The people in the back rows sing
Rock of Ages
the family gives the last look in,
my mother (no one above her now)
kisses the lips cold as stone.
Around the dirt the dark hats of farmers' wives
bob and shake and stiffen,
the city backs of men in long grey coats
are straight against the cold.
Separation occurs and then
up in my room I am waiting for it to enter me
house and brothers quiet yet all like a web
that a stone
falls through: winter winds clean away
the flower stench but
I am still walking, walking in bare-legged silence
pitching stones at
roadside roses, tearing holes in leaves.

DEATH OF THE VIOLIN

. . . in our house came after four years.
She had practiced—and not practiced—
long enough to (finally) make music.
She had entertained my father and mother,
and I had been proud of the songs
she had coaxed from those harsh strings.
She was, however, not staying with it.
We could no longer continue with
reminders, because reminders would be
nagging, and we wanted discipline
on her part: we wanted her to bring her will
into play.

November is a hard month to give up anything,
especially if you have held it
four years, watched it grow in your arms
until you knew just how
to make the music leap.
My own father's violin hangs on the wall
and I remember when he played,
touching strings, jabbing
at the notes until the instrument
became a fiddle, and around him
guitars and accordions
filled up the family with their talk.

Once when she played,
his violin played back,
reverberating on the wall: just once
that calling note. Then silence
filled up now with rain.
Arguments about who's supporting whom
fade, but stay, fill the air,

can't move gently into change.
And someone's disclaiming all reason
and another's volume rises to the shriek.

APHASIA

It is the suddenness of crossing
over
that cannot be comprehended.
One moment she is among us
reaching for her purse . . .

The nurses clean and cuddle,
talk numbers—
b.p. one-ten-over-sixty—
and these we babble to friends
and those givers of ill advice,
hours when the smells are
not our own, even children
quietening down
in the sudden blow of dumbness
where she lives.

After a journey of many simplicities
we see her still
alone, at a great distance, immobile
behind that other number
none can guess. We practice
contact
but she cannot

at first   we smash up
inside   all night
after the hours of visitation have safely
passed and the dark leads us
away. Alone on the ward
she hunts for *bed*
car   teeth   comb

DAVID DALE

Forced to abandon him
by a grade one teacher who could not accept
two boys with the same name, I accepted
my second. I think of David
as a skin dropped, a ball
lost in the summer grass.

My parents often spoke of him
or mouthed my new name
as if I were a guest
and they were waiting politely
for his return

—because what faults I had
could never spring from him.
Well, did he grow up
through change, embarrassment,
and try to speak the lines
reserved after all for him? He never did.

When I meet him now
at dawn or just before sleep, he stands
speechless although I know he wants from me
more than words.

Lately, when I cut myself
on paper, and the sharp red line wells over
and falls, his young mouth
is pressed against my hand.

HERE ON THE COAST

. . . it is the dead
who speak to us
from the water
and from the trees.

Dark inlet,
you invite me under,
you keep saying
another waits.

Since we know
water alone
cannot speak so clearly
whose dead

does the sojourner
hear? His own,
made precious by absence?
The ones who call to him
always when he comes near water?

Or some other
who mistakes his melancholic
way for a heart.

Then the trees call:
from their bases,
fluted mouths to the ground,
they are taking up
into the sky

their entangling love
of the air.

FATHER'S WORK

When he was home,
he was absent. And yet
several summers now dead,
he still sends love
back over that line
I've kept alive for him
in the far western
corner of a thought and along which
I will someday also vanish.

So it was work he fled to:
he pulled animals off one another
when they fought and tangled.
He killed and emptied the pig
and set in motion my
imagination: beside the wet entrails
the rocks on the ground shone,
colourful intestines
I called gut-stones
and for years half believed
a father's force
turned flesh directly into gems.

I myself go to an office, a room,
but he went outside, machines
needing a patch or thrust
into flame.
Now I'd take his hand,
lead him to a table
where my children spread paintings,
and ask him to contemplate
men and women who seem always
to be striking off the page.

Where are they going, I ask.
Where can I intercept them
and get them to rest?

I reach for more tasks
to help avoid
the unpleasantness that rises
sometimes from leisure
—and I think of his Sunday:
he reached out and made stillness,
urged animal and family
to join in reflecting
the moment a soul
once born is born again.
Wife, sons, horse, dog,
the claw of the hammer,
the blade of the scythe
thus prepared for Monday,
its arc upward into the long life
I'm pushing through right now,
both far and not far from
the nights we sank and never moved,
brothers with the stones
appearing in the moonlit fields
after each passing
of our father's plough.

MY MOTHER'S WAIL

When guests first came to our house
—young women destined to wed
into our family—we warned them
Mum might wail in the part of the night
when we had no chance to hold off
what drifted through the house,
up the stairs to the beds where
we lay, suddenly awake, our hearts
ringing up our brains
frozen by her long vowel
—uuu—unformed by tongue
as it came straight up from
inside my mother where we didn't
think anyone ever lived.

Next morning we joked, and Mother
laughed, no longer embarrassed,
for she herself had never heard
the ur-sound she made, had only
once or twice caught a little
of its end when Dad rolled close
and shook her back to us. He said
we should record her
and make a bundle, and once,
I planned to go to her when next
that moan rolled from her slack mouth,
to comfort her as she would surely
comfort me, but when the time came
I did not, could not, for fear
that who I heard would wake
and be someone other than my mum.

Sometimes I see her
flannel nightgown on the stairs
and in her arms extra blankets for
the night. She tucks in all who
shelter under her roof, she stokes
the fire last, checks
doors, glances in on sleeping forms,
sends her prayers up through
rafters and on to the stars
and then settles with
her dark and starts the roving
back through day and week;
and year after year the speed
of moving becomes a falling
in which she cries out to us.

There seems to be no gene for wailing
passed on to us, no
nightly crying out of our miserable selves
to frighten those around us,
and yet I fear some sound
out of us so low as to be
below the normal pitch of voice,
toneless ululating
close to the beginning
of sound that keeps with it
a realm I never could
imagine by daylight through in the dark
I saw too well what halts and waits
inside my mother's shell.

A STORY

After six months I put the ring
back on and found once again
that it fit, that it could pass over
the fat part of the finger
and rest comfortably next to
the palm with its criss-cross
of lines someone other than me
might read to discover my destiny.
It's shining there now, a thing
of good gold, and when I ponder
past and future, I fiddle it round
and my eye can catch its gleaming
edge. So perhaps after all I did

lose weight although I still feel
winded running behind my plans,
and when I stand naked after bath
with that body in full light,
I see where life has packed itself on
in every minute of overtime—
and now I've added this ring,
a few ounces to lighten up
the hand. You did notice

right away, and asked why,
and right away I said
the ring no longer grips tight
but almost the way it felt
when a simple adornment on the left
could announce a change has come
into the world and here was its
symbol: continuity of the finest stuff,
not something we might hammer
out one night.

So after these months of ours
I find a form that fits, new now
as continuing to live
after a birth or death is new.
Whichever it is, I often pause
to think. But my hands refuse
change, want still to gather in flesh
which then must be released back to you
so you can fight my need
—hard at work in me—
to forge around you a circle
of my old ways, not exactly
that fabulous place where gold
is broken and mended seamlessly
or produced out of substance far more
fragile than straw.

HOW I JOINED HUMANITY AT LAST

When love
in the heart speaking to me
dies out, I walk
the street to be near
men and women who recognize
the death in me.

Instead I see the death in them:
in that man's eyes a wound
glows through; this woman
loves a man
whose body turned away.
They could make no deal
to sidestep pain for the sake of
a good night's sleep, for
comfort and companionship
so regret
will not cut so deeply in years ahead
that it might kill.

I look for signs: a scrap of paper
on the street, the word
that will start me off again.
Instead I see
those I did not see before
who want from me
what none of us can give.
We turn away, and later
can only bear a very little violence
on TV, and later still,
awakened in our beds
with nothing but the clock to say
time has not yet passed,

our hearts turn
terrorist, aflame
in the two a.m. nightmare
with its need for vengeance
—and its sword of dismay.

THE EXHAUSTED PAST

Where did you go wrong
that you ended up
with this worthless life?
You could say anything here,
and it would not matter.

The exhausted past
tires you, so don't mumble on,
except to say you have read as many books
as the maple had leaves,
now flaring yellow into red
as if even the tree wishes to make
a clean break—and when it stands
in the winter wind and rain,
is that perhaps the necessary triumph
admitting spring?
Organic images! Soon each word
inside your books begins to assume
the shape of hope, the position
of the bean before it sprouts and curls upward
into the sky through thick
and thin and into clouds, a good place
to jump from,

glide down from—
wings appearing just as you need them
to make yourself renew again
what the years before
did to you, how they
reduced you to a crouch,
which you fall away from
even as the river rises to meet first your hands
held together in the piercing position of prayer
and then your lips, your streaming hair,
the one shoe that stayed with you.

REASONS FOR LIVING

. . . start with my children,
the way they carry air
into my rooms and make the windows
want to fly open
so the dining-room
daffodils raise their bent necks
and open their faces, speechless but full.
But no child can keep me
from my thinking
and I try the earth itself,
the smell of the green ravine,
the ruby-crowned kinglet
dancing in the buds of the conifers,
his wings never still,
until one evening he says to me,
"What's the matter with you?
Isn't it enough that I'm here?
You want to be me, is that it?
You want transformation?"
He's gone, and when I take a plant, later,
from the ravine, bring it here
into my life, I know
it can offer
only green and nothing more
when the light goes out.
But for the time I bend
in sweat and gently tear it
up from its world,
I have no thought,
I do not see myself,
I fill myself fully to the edges.
I know the edges are beginning
to fray, one hole already big enough
to fly a blackbird through,

slip a hand through, not mine
for they are busy grubbing,
but it could be a hand
of a lover I once had,
or a child that has grown while I slept.

THE WAY PAST WORDS

Under the hands of the massage therapist
I begin to let go
of my old life
lodged in flesh.
Sadness arises out of my back and neck
and enters my thinking
without words. Then I
leave behind that soft flannel
table where for a moment
I was new, my throat working.
I walk where young men
bend their bodies for tools,
and I stop to imagine
who will fill the spaces
they are building. I see
a man who ponders his books,
feels fine in his work
and in the company of others, but then
his own conversations tell him
not to bother, he will not find
the way past words
into undivided being.
Two blocks later
I come to rest again
at the bottom of my voice,
in the grip of the words
most fundamentally mine.
So I turn back and
ask for her firmest hand
to reach through the sinews
and find what once served well;
once, but no more. Her hand
meets resistance; inch by inch,

deal-making, she pulls
from my chest this
child, a gnome grinning
as if he is seeing
the sun beyond death.
We watch as he speaks
and begins to age.
If she returns him to me
through the power of her hands
—pressing him back through my spine—
will I become suddenly
myself in the space between peace
and the words for peace?
Or fall instead into the heart
pounding for all that is nameless?

THE BEAUTIFUL VOICE OF THE UNDERTAKER

. . . rises from the last pew
to help carry the frail body
of the old woman
away from her family, his tenor
carrying over us all, not
showing off or even showing the way

and those of us not caught up in
the moment as it flashes
and is gone
could tell he has sung this song
before, and yet he sings also

for this woman,
to the soul which he could only
have known from her body,
and because his voice is strong
we can suppose—can we not—
he feels grief.

Now as he straightens his back
and opens his heart to the hymn
his own mother
fills the kitchen
with the sweet lift of soprano
on a Saturday afternoon when he himself

was too tired
to break out the games
or find his companions at the edge
of the woods, and so he sat there
in his own dreamy life,
and the cinnamon buns

and the warm milk in the jar
held him still and made him think
and when he asked her
she turned and was not fast
like sometimes she could be:
you will be a violinist one day

—and he took that and changed it
to the man who blew the strong
sad notes at the end of the movie,
he would be the one who made tears,
and even he could not understand
why sadness should be a desire

—and so he came to sing at funerals
not in any showy way
but as a voice we could follow
when he carried sorrow out the door into
the woods and laid it down
among the roots and leaves.

THE MAN WHO INVENTED THE TURN SIGNAL

The man who invented the turn signal
walks out the factory gates
somewhere in the west
knowing he's done a service
to the world hitting the road
by telling the car behind

it's turning; we speak
as if the car has brains and eyes
—and the man who invented the turn signal
knows he should just listen to
the meadowlarks
now he's out the gates

but his mind keeps
going on, turning over
itself in all the corners
in order to make the signal
come back to neutral
on its own.

Already he has foreseen
a young woman driving a convertible—
she forgets to pull her signal off
so forever after she is turning
and all the cars behind her,
all the young men who follow her

go off in directions she isn't going—
she keeps looking straight ahead.
Our man imagines that woman needs
him, wants his arm to reach over
and gently flick the signal back
and maybe she smiles

or thanks him
with her eyes, the blue
he'll wake to some day, some place
he'd fix up for her, not
the bungalow he's in now,
he should be wealthy as can be:

he invented
the simple and worthwhile, so the future
won't give a thought to it,
he's already done that,
arriving at last
at that little rubber wheel

the bigger steering wheel rubs and
slowly nudges back into place
with the brilliance of plain devising,
he could show her how it works,
draw her attention to his genius, then
gently drop his hand on hers,

so cool on the wheel even though
it was warm as sunny could be,
so much stretching out
between one meadowlark and another,
and the gift
of all those poles along the road, each one

saying *call me, you can call me,*
if I've ever wanted to love a man
it would have to be someone like you,
someone who has brains and hands
like yours, good at signals
I can pick up along the road.

This is the 1950s,
they come to love in a tender way;
everything can happen
almost does. Best of all
their children are golden
from the sun.

THE OWL

Last night I twisted up the sheets,
my arm trapped by my side
where it throbbed and then sprang

free, to push open the window
for some air and—there, half-
awake, I heard the owl

Fogged up in dreams of roads
I was afraid to walk, I had no
will, I heard notes hard to

catch, harder to remember,
a first big hoot and then three
short sounds, the last almost

musical as it trailed off
and hinted he would not call
again, his night-work done,

and then twice more he called
and I lay in my tangled bed
and tried hard to be awake

tried hard to be alive in case
he called one more time and
I understood what he said

MY FIRST JOB

The job descends on me
from my father cutting the grass
with his scythe, through my mother
bent over the peas and tossing
weeds where cows take a tongueful
or leave them for the heat
passing over my brothers
home late at night with dollars
in their pockets and up early
to lean into sweat, the job
of killing the kittens
comes down to me

I lure the mother cat away
with fresh cream
and then lift the young up
before their eyes are open
and they look through smoky lenses
and make me fail
the farm overrun, never enough mice
to keep them healthy

and ours not a home
to feed cats more than
milk shot at their wet and open
mouths straight from the cow
or a splash
spilled in an old dish
they lick clean
before going back out
to leap at swallows
dive-bombing their furious tails

I panic at the last
when I stuff them in the sack
and feel their five
bodies tiny as organs twitching
against the burlap—I have already
dug the hole, twisting down
the post-hole digger two feet
then three, and I remember
my mother has drowned one batch
and thinking I can repeat

such a feat, I throw them
into their hole and dump in a pail
of water, but see instead how fast
it flows through the sack
and sand and is gone
the bundles wet, more visible
in their plungings
until I throw on the dirt
again and again and then whack

the ground with the back
of the shovel, and leave that place
and leave the tools for later
to be picked up later, after
I return to the barn to see
the one I left for the mother
looking at the mother's wild eyes
when I approach, seeing
the one I spared, marvelling
at the choice I made

the ground I made holy
and will avoid
for days, weeks, noting never
to dig in that spot, thinking
as I call the dog for our
walk out of the yard and away
to the field, of the tasks
my mother and father carried out
in their obligations year
after year, how much they could do
and not change

DREAM

I am in a desert,
the nearest man
far away
on the horizon
and when I reach him
he is talking about himself
his burden made for me to hear
his time so brief
or too long
that my dream
—when Death bites me
in the front right shoulder—
goes unsaid

Next I am on a bridge
in creek therapy,
a couple walking past
speaking a language I know
though it isn't mine
his bass presentation of the plan
her high complaint
that yet says yes

I want to speak into a space
the way a wild bird calls
into air, note after note from the tree
those sounds I hear
in dreams
when birds come to murmur
of the blue pool in the ravine

a feather drifting, this way, that
the spot on the ground not often
if ever
preordained, the white bird
passing on

EDGE

I walk along the window ledge
with ease although below
I see in the minds looking up
that notable image of Icarus
tipping into the sea
feathers useless above him

which pigeons, here, have shed
mostly grey, curled, fluffy
easily blown in the wind except when
they're stuck by excrement
which I step over
in my quest to walk the length

I have caused concerns
to rise up from below
Yesterday I was one of them
I have worried myself
but they will not stop me
from advancing along
my toes finding every hold

An hour ago I put down
my pencil, stepped to the window
felt all my strength return
as I pushed up the sash
turned once to say goodbye
eased my weight out

my hands like suckers against
the wall, my leather soles smooth
on the slightly inclined edge
But it was my shirt that filled
with wind, my hair that lifted

METHOD

"He never could tell when his heart might drop again
and leave him unable to remember any need to do
anything."
—A.L. Kennedy, "True"

I come to the steps of the old house
in the park looking for
an exact anger
that once found and felt
will lead to the next
exact anger and the next.
But here the sun's afternoon angle
promises more than heat,
its language
warmly metaphoric,
its trees casting long
layers of light
on the lawn
and the beginning evening breeze
brings a child's taunt:
"Paul is a baby! Paul is a baby!"
and a father's voice
raised: "Yes, it will stay;
now leave it." Reasons for living
I'll deal with later
after this moment
turns its thoughts toward
the questions of overcoming
attachment, but listen
here is where some of you
should disembark, having tasted
sweat along my lids
which a hot afternoon has placed there

not from walking and working up
those fit feelings of physical righteousness
but from the shakier inside working
its way out and staining a reader's
forward view with a colour not too nice—
so off with you, then!—and no blame,
but if you stay with me now,
you've given up the right
to speak against
the soft-sentence version
of what is felt: the will
to energy
dead, the natural
turn of the mind
caught in a cant
out of fashion but right at home
as if I'd been reared by folks different
from those home-going, lawn-crossing ones
their bats and balls and towels
announcing father's less cross
if he knows light this time of day
illumines with Disney
clarity but gives as well the gift of air
to create dimension; no, I've been raised
on the Prussian principle of bold stinginess,
wind from the plains
cold when I for one
wish to lie close
not to another but to the ground
where I can name the flies
that buzz me. But first
a tour! Of my neighbourhood,
so you, determined reader,

can see where I walk
these streets,
perhaps to spy your house
or an old couple passing by;
a baby's arms, open to summer,
branching from its sides: pink
cactus; then a fat, blond child

wet from the sprinkler,
thin polyester PJs
clinging to her skin: she digging at
some sliver in her bulging hand
fully focused until she swerves
her gaze onto me; the biker
clattering up the street and rolling
his machine across the sidewalk
to be welcomed home
by the hollyhocks
tall as the shapeless house they hide,
the gas tank of his bike
dressed in purple teardrops
like dashes of blood
slanting back in the wind
from hands held high
to grip the reins;
the oldest man on the block still pushes
his mower up the slope of his walk and
when he looks up
he's grimace and teeth:
what an old, hard-working smile
looks like; the guy
in green shorts, pink top
stretches tight its little

alligator—not afraid to bend down
and stick his bum in the street
as he picks at the weeds
near his toes; Jenn Scott's
name on a yellow symbol
of a fish at the entrance
to a street-drain to warn us
we must not pour down death,
must not play God.
So if it's anger we come to
on this trek, it's not the flash
that burns out the sky and consumes
the undeniable end of things
in the plunge toward what's coming our way
but can't be seen on the usual size screens
most of us are watching;
more like the slow drip
of generation into generation
that helps me clean
the bathroom, and the rest of the apartment
can wait. A billionaire from Hong Kong
has bought the building but I can move,
I'm on the top floor
and I can fly. I've phoned one daughter
to say I love her
and she said in return
she loved me—and the exchange
was easeful and true;
the younger one I've helped
out of a jam: neighbour's gone away
and she volunteered to take on
their cat—feeding, petting: prevention
to keep it from going wild,

rumoured to be its response
to prolonged abandonment;
smart move, I'd say. So
I'm full of daily events, some
secretly life-giving, drawing sweetness
out of me, as my spider-grass
kinks its leaf one day
and sends out a bud
to meet the potential
bane that can come
to new blooms. Imagine my children
coming upon me flat on the floor,
red in the tub:
what they would carry
the moment a word went in
and hatched, stayed with them
through the first
anniversary, the second, the memory
transfiguring itself, a living stalk
sending out its own runners to creep
and trap and hold back
natural joy until it was gone.
You picture this, patient reader,
no doubt imagine this lot
on yourself at least once,
not among those
who never give in to a thought
that curves and takes on
a life of its own.
You and I took extra shots in the womb
of Daddy's zest.
Mummy's heart beating
always here, here, here

and when we bother with beyond
for a moment alone
before sun-up or at night
—not for long—what we hear
is soon enough gone, drowned
by blood rushing eardrums
and the simple surprise of
what the eye can find
even in the dark: the clock beams
on the bookcase, the curtains
reveal a night breeze; trees
strong as grandfathers
draw us back into sleep,
and our dreams
are not clutter out of which
comes the next day's crush.
And walking through the neighbourhood
—still with me?—I look for
one stark thought I can clash against
but recall instead how
something leaked into me
from the gene pool, tightened
each day a little more
until I was shrink-wrapped
and laughable, the skin around my face
pulled down, my exoskeleton self
not too good either. I worried
I was missing what all other men
seemed to have: themselves
and a way of walking
through the mall that said:
Milady, I have the most amazing balls
loaded for your pleasure and your kin

and I can compose your two-note song
on the linen so sweetly
that you give me
a moment I go blank
and in rushes love, out bolts
the mud-blood—
and the books from smiling people
tell how to cope.
I'm reading in the mall;
I glance up
to the mirror above the bestsellers, to see
my unbelievable look: grumpy,
cagey, selfy, silly,
woody, wobbly and dick.
I close the book and return to
checking faces as they go by: that mouth
plunges, this mouth (all straight
across but pulling up) stays in place
wanting a bargain that will
give hope to hope—and where
does he bury his rage in his cat,
his car, his sport, his wife,
his secret hand, food,
his lawn? which we are passing now,
green gem that signals to the universe
its code of order, boxer shorts,
tools arranged on the downstairs wall,
and a dream far off, speeding out to Mars
it's like that for all of us
some time: we stop believing
our own stories and get
wild that our selves
didn't work, that not enough people

felt good to us long enough,
that it was just us
everywhere in our consciousness
and that everyone else was just them;
and in the moment of surrender
after waking when I am without words
and only images
flock around, without my story,
I am naked, inconsolable, under attack,
self-indulgent—yet most myself?
I wake and before the words begin
three doors marked
pain, pain, pain
wait to be opened.
In what night was I deemed
its carrier? Was there a congregation
of beings, lights, flashes,
that touched my father's shoulder
and turned to my mother
for entry? How much can I lay
at their bedside,
those big humans
—yet sometimes what I see
is love: their goof-waltzing
in the kitchen, better than their
smooth displaying
dance in town;
and sometimes what I see is dark and grim
as they took bad weather
on the chin and fell in
on themselves—
we all get a knock on the head.
I look at my father's

burning, the more constant less
spectacular show of my mother's flame,
what they had to work with
and what they worked against
and how they were in their lives
and how mine was not
headquarters,
how irreparable
my one-ness got to be
as I grew up and they did not
—and while I often think now
of laughter, card games
at a good volume of life,
what comes through
is grieving
that the wholeness of promise
could not blitz fears;
and the arc of their lives
is the arc of every life
including mine, and the variations
don't count
before the pattern
we rail against,
stepping on and off the story-line
and by fancy-dancing
hope to feel truly
what is
and what is dying.
Reasons for living
come later, as does perspective
and humour, and even the arts
of steeling oneself nicely,
but not now, not right now

in your head: you
fall away, nothing's holding up,
others have nets by now,
their groups, smiles
and ways of taking an eyeful of death
and still winging on.
Yes, love makes light,
love meets the day.
Love can hold you
in the night like a good song says.
Love can find you or not.
I'll okay this version anyway,
okay these irritations,
poisons, pleasures
—needs, one to walk
and walk, discover I am
not the successful community member
but what the neighbourhood needs:
he who passes a drift bit of talk
and constructs a life, the smells
of kitchens, the call of kids;
and out on the field
at Fen Burdett Stadium the young men
love to play baseball in the rain,
it makes them stronger, more real,
beer better at the end,
and if questions arise,
at least tired muscles soon
pull the brain into sleep.
I'm telling you
things you don't want to know
about another person, I'm saying
in this age we all want

one finger in some wound
and will travel the world
to find the right one. I know
the age of confession has passed,
is passé, but my friends
can't bear to listen
and so, reader, you are my confessor,
only you can hear me out
and I reach for you across the page
and pull you in, let me do it,
I've got an ache
you can make better
just by taking me in—and you know
we're all feeling snarled though
many of us are tough
for the sake of
others around us. Run your tongue
over the morbid
and the mean, the little hole
at the edge of the hairline
out of which you fly.
But where does "I" go
if anywhere and who to believe if anyone
and why not wait to find out later?
And so, as they say,
most of my healing is done
at night, and these exaggerations
I rise up from Woolco sheets to embrace,
preferably with a flourish
that gives meaning
or at least the strength of meaning
further on in the day. Yes,
I can feel it now

yearning in me
as I look high up into the face of the
Molecule—could be, you know
since one by one they are replaced,
the electrons that sing in me
their little steady hymn
get trucked away
into the blood, and new ones
arise unmanufactured
to walk the same race.
Do you recall walking this way—
with such thoughts in your head?
And I'm by your side
pointing out the way it looks:
a nightmare here
and over there a sinking heart
we were not prepared for,
a lump of coal growing
in your lover's breast,
a June
wet and ungiving
waiting to be cleaned off
my files, drawing my attention
to please note
I'm still flying
on the propulsion
of my last life crisis: so zoom
I live, and live.

WHAT TO DO

I am trying to get it all done.
Not just the nails and hair and teeth
of my body that demands
me in the morning
and then in the night as if it were
two different bodies, each wanting
a life of its own rid of
the counterpart that drags
away from the pure clean
drive of the moment—
and where the body lives
clothes need laying out
and cleaning, dust gathers
and can't be gotten rid of for good
it's so persistent
the way other entities are not:
money health love
while the dust reminds me
time is being used up
falling on the geraniums
and on the photographs
on my face as I sleep and sometimes
dream of a place where
deeds once done
stay permanently held
and formed and without
their little voices to cry out
for my attention when I waltz past
on my way to one further task
already risen to the topmost
of the lost, at least on the list
that gets scratched down, not
the lost I avoid

except when, my upper head
opens wide and out rushes
the urge that insists
I climb onto memory and
tamp down and rearrange
until it's part of things
—and I get beyond such thinking
with the little business of going
down the stairs and into the air
to notice how the car shines
how fast it can take me
down the road, the sweet feelings
of leaving behind
the dust with its claim
so unlike my shoes and scarves
my gloves in the hall
the anorak awaiting weather
all so clear they never allow me
to confuse sun with hail
or a drift of blossoms with snow.

PRAYER FOR A FRIEND

He bore the mark of the knife
on the back of his head,
an inverted u like the print
of a horseshoe where the surgeon
had entered his brain and removed
a class 4
malignant tumour that had already
taken peripheral vision on the left.
I couldn't help but look
at the shaved patch
with its metal stitches, my eye
drawn there, as a tongue
inserts itself into a cavity.

We talked of past and future,
with words only friends can use
—terminal, tomorrow,
radiation, memory—and I found
my fingers were digging on their own
into the fabric of the blanket
covering the couch: they found holes
in the knotty
knitted material. I need to dig
and cling, thinking of his wife
in the kitchen, making a pale tea.

My cornea is distorted by the steroids,
he says, and so the house
is full of people; he sees one now
sitting between us, a young boy
from the '50s, clean and strong
as if this is an angel of his
former self come to bring him love,
not just electrical hallucinations,
not mere emanations from his need
to keep his spirit strong.

On the drive home I go through
a red light. No one runs into me.
I hit no one. I pull to the curb, panting
a bit, my hands fighting the wheel.
It comes down to this:
I am lucky. Sometimes it happens that way,
my own angel directing everyone
to tasks that take them elsewhere.
Dear angel, I promise to look out more—
thank you and now, please, I release you
from your charge of me so you may
fly to my friend and touch his head.

CROWS DO NOT HAVE RETIREMENT

"There are no words to capture the infinite depth of
crowiness in the crow's flight."
—Ted Hughes, *Winter Pollen*

Crows do not have retirement
homes to go to when finally
their wings break down

No one takes them in
with a sigh and says
sit here for a bit

while I bring you
a cup of raw worm
to help keep your head

swivelling, on the lookout
for fledglings or the dead,
the eagle making you

flock and dive
that white untouchable pate
No one guides them gently

into their last years,
takes account of their
final movements or hears

their calls, their stout beaks
opening without sound
as if thirsting,

their inky heads against
the starchy white linen,
constant television nearby

They fold up in the curb
in the August heat,
the sheen gone from wings

they no longer lift
out of the heap
no other crow will touch

nor even admit,
passing by without
an exploratory peck

leaving their own kind
to gulls, rats, worms, the municipality
To keep the black

ideal of ravenousness
alive, they hop and lift off
and cruise past windows

where old men catch their flash
and are sent off dreaming
of their own unequalled speed and grace

the guns they once held
in their long arms and the damage
they shook from the air

THE OPTIONS

When you die
here are the options:
everything or oblivion

A centre of light and around it
all you love, those dead
and those abiding still
and each holding
an object of endearment
you lost long ago
before you came to
know and be simultaneously
at last
at rest
beyond words

Or else your cells
stop their chemical
talk, the neurons say no
and their warmth leaves you
not with black
not even the absence of black—
nothing of earth's up, round, biomass, span
just the non-existence
you tried to conjure once
by closing your eyes and
sleeping, except that dreams
fired their figments
across space at you
and your muscles straining

While we live
we pick one of these options
to live by, and neither is understood
the way the robin in the tree is
who speaks to us of March lust,
the way water and clouds are
which tells us to walk out
into the day, how to step
on grass and mud and feel the pull
upward and then sag an hour later
down, we with our little time
and our ideas and our blood

HOW I CAME TO BE

1.

One March night my folks
took themselves to bed
and found inside their comfort
some love left
She curled after
picturing a daughter to complement
two sons and one girl already
behind other walls, asleep
He flung his arm
and drifted, seeing chores
that lay ahead, the seeding
far enough away to contemplate
with pleasure because this season
was still long although
yesterday he had seen the first crow
and felt his mood lift

But what of *me* between
these two: why pick them
from among the multitudes
meeting and begetting that very night
(an early morning tilt when a freight
banged by and half-awoke
two slippery reaching dreamers
or the tired sore workers
who found nothing but this moment
of sharing and saying wild words
to steady them for one more shift
or the young, young pretty ones
whose trembling bore them
past that point they had so often

been forewarned about
—history now, sad or otherwise
is hard yet to say)
Instead I came here, to these limbs
this farm, these white fields
swept with a snaky wind

2.

All that summer my mother
carried me through the heat
and when I recognized winter again
by the soft slow nights
I knew it was time to show them
who I was

although I could not reveal
who I had been
before I materialized that night
taking spirit handfuls from each:
his ears, her heart

        —but from neither
my need for snow: that was my own
desire, that would be the tiny bit
I carried on my own—

        and my first
and frequent cries that followed
kept them from fretting
about the cold, remembering always
to press me near and warm

Only now and then was I left
by the window where ice
leapt with the draft upon the pane
into filaments of shine and angle
recalling I could be
no longer
that cool bright light of
almost emptiness so entirely
filled with more than me

HAD I STAYED ON THE FARM

for Leona Gom

I married the skinny girl
and our kids ran free as chickens
one of them, the second boy
moving along the ditches for days
trapping muskrat and living on
chokecherries and bulrushes
sleeping by a little fire of sticks
wrapped in his jacket, and we hardly noticed
he was gone until he returned
as someone else, burnt and smoky
his sisters silenced by the strides he took
to reach the pump, the way he drank
from the barn well, his hands
a mesh of little nicks and cuts
where the cries of the animals
had entered him

I planted, and prayed
for the market to hold, and when
it failed I stopped praying
and never began again
found a fount of colourful
language when the truck broke
at harvest—and when the green straw plugged
the combine, I was the fool
who crawled in, it was my mackinaw
the flywheel caught and drove hard
into the iron guts of the machine
it was the mangled me my son
found, his mother he ran to
but even before he reached her
with the news she ever after

kept hearing, kept hearing
all the black suits of my neighbours
on their hangers
at the backs of the closets
thirsting for sun and wind

I knew little of books
nothing of rhyme
though the rhythm
of spring, summer, fall
I replayed in winter
every day a time
for breaking down and
making each moment all
I needed, the snow filling up
space I might have stuffed otherwise
with words or lies or worse
falling until all was smooth
and white, virgin
cold
beauty I eventually forgot
to see, seeing instead
lives I might have lived
had I left, had I taken the train
not taken, riding with those
who later returned with ironic gleams
to look at me in wonder, the one
who stayed, as if only one were needed
to rate themselves against
measuring me as their fathers measured
fields of chaff and shrivelled grain

JAPANESE MALLOW

When the inevitability of my mortality
overwhelms me momentarily, I . . .
touch these repeating pink blossoms
their delicacy softens self-sorrow
makes dying a mere event among lives
continuing to thrive: those bolstering me
(not by bluster) by showing how, exemplars
of one-who-calms-down, fathers who help
finish homework, moms with nightly rhymes
also *you* I've never met, who know me
as sentences, not an entirely true reproduction
but close, the way wind grasps petals it takes
to drop first here and then far
from the tilting, un-mournful mother plant

POSTCARD FROM ITALY

Tonight I am approaching Italy again
down from the Alps, the long tunnels behind
    now the gravel beds and rivers intertwined
    with light and square high towers on plains
where trees march like infantry, in perfect rows
across a hill humped like a Roman nose

it's late spring, I stand by marble ruins and think
of the years softened, sent away by this sun:
    at Aquileia, the aqueduct has come undone
    stone by stone and now shrinks
among the grass and poppies, a wild rabbit leaping
through a field of wheat, the south wind sweeping

its living green, more living than the hand
that made stones rise—and at flat-calm Adriatic's shore
    I scoop thin grey sand and pour
    its dust along the wet edge, where land
goes under sea; and then that light again, suddenly felt
again, a madonna's light, and winter-me melts

HOW BRAVE

"... make a complete exit from life, not in anger, but
simply, freely, with integrity, making this leaving of it
at least one achievement in your life."
—Marcus Aurelius, *Meditations*

How brave of a worldly one dying
on his white antiseptic bed to say
there is no god and I have become death
his last breath a final simple heaving
not extending upwards into arms
of waiting deities, his forehead damp
not with excitement or exaltation
but effort of animal exertion that must
be borne, yes, and thus he suffers
the magnitude of the task, of leaving
corporeal substance, the scrabbling hand
and even what's called consciousness
the flame that asks always why *is*
feels both unborn and deathless

How bravely those who cannot believe
meet the moment when an afterlife
begins for others, not them, and how
they stay stoic, having learned ways
not to hope or despair—denying either—
but to penetrate the mystery of the day
in mornings when they live clear-headed
—in afternoons they sag, work-logged—
in evenings when they stop to weigh
the stars, imagining not so much
themselves arriving as dust from such
a distance, nor being small beyond
meaning itself—just breathing hearts
beating numbers, recognizing time

How brave to die when we can't behold
our parents arriving to greet our souls
embarking apparently from pale beds where
we fight for the dignity of our aloneness
though clustered around by attendant
machines and our bewildered children
How we have raged for our right not to be
herded by churchy cherubs, not to further
cosmic harmonics in our progression from
matter toward what can hardly be said
To enter rot and raise no arm and shout!
To prepare our gratitude and give back
without benefit of flood or inferno, wordlessly
what we borrowed in our mothers' wombs

HOW TO WALK IN THE DARK WITH FLOWERS

Open your eyes to the light
in the armful of lilies you are holding

Move forward and be guided
by the sheen of their white curves
quavering stamens of dizzy gold
shimmering back at you as you

take the first step
A torch of flower-light
does not allow itself
to feel
cut from the earth
Just think: to be beautiful
and dying at the same, last time

Lay the lilies down on the body
Leave them, and say goodbye

Now, groping along
on hands and knees
the help you need
you generate yourself
as you wait for lucidity
to descend
with its burden
of resolve

which you'll readily embrace, arms eager
glad to push upright again
dark clay at a good distance
wind from the sky heaping around you
living aromas
from beings of light someone planted
many years ago

RAISED WITH DOGS

"Most good poets recognize the corked wine and
fall silent."
—Conor O'Callaghan

Because I was raised with dogs I've seen
their glum look as they enter a certain age
just as I'd watched horses wait long hours
in the shade of poplars, slowly switching
silken tails while nearby snakes split the grass
cats pounce on voles, children cavort
and mystify their parents with their lies

Bright trees wave in wind and then drop
one night all their leaves and thereafter
are silent, revealing themselves as
mere twigs strung together for a nest
where a gawkling crept from a shell
and was pushed, stumbled off its edge
into space, and when spring pressed
his breast open, then he sang and sang

Miles beyond all this unfolding nature
(and unnatural unfolding: boys wicked
with weaner pigs, girls gone slow
around their winking porky uncles)
down the dusty road and into the CNR
station, along wooden boards, up
into steam and iron working a whistle
he's taken to a destination: afternoon irony
coffee clashes, knowledge on display

and later with the solitary wine
tasting cork bits bobbing in the glass
that he tips back, knowing dismay
because he cannot return, reverse
to what he was, that dash of time
among willows, watching wild ducks
float in dignity far from alarming land—
and ahead his dogged look deepening
nothing worth howling about but howling
nonetheless, refusing to whimper
holding back silence with a warning bark

THE FLY IN AUTUMN

Yes, the light
    once more
        comes down
                at last
through clouds
to warm my blue ass
here on the yet-green nettle leaf, summer
near the bear plop, and we the species
best at finding dung, in this end light
or in the glow of an early planet

And even so, my wings
carry me, and what thinness
upon which to rely

SINKING

One morning he woke up and started sinking
down through flannel sheets, through foam
through each airspace in foam, his fingers
clutching what he kept missing, missing it
when he opened his hand, nothing there and
the same nothing kept with him as he sank

down through cloth, coils and then
through his parquet floor, and he panicked
when he entered the ceiling of those
who lived below—but they were workers
and they had already left, their bed sheets
untidy, and he couldn't help noting

pants on the floor, a tube of lipstick tipped
on the dresser, its lid off, the living colour
alarmingly red, and he descended
through shag rug musty with crumbs
and unswept hairs, sock fuzz, toenails
and once a glitzy button passed by

He began to relax now he knew he could
manage ceilings and floors, believing
he would stop when he met hard earth
so down through six discrete floors
he fell, slowly, almost as one drifting, not
plummeting, not a disaster, just a descent

He waved goodbye to operational apparatus
in the basement and then easily entered
concrete and felt the first brisk cold muscle
of buried earth so long removed from light
and incalescence, and knew he would continue
until he met the central fire of the globe

and he wondered if heat at the heart
would be his final immolating destination
if that forge would provide the brake
he needed—but already he was thinking
it hardly mattered where he finally ceased
because the journey toward heat would be

long, long, much longer than six floors
and he would need to settle into accepting
this fate if he wanted any clear mind left
when he came face to face with molten flame
calling him, undoubtedly calling, though last night
he could not have imagined any such sound

SOMEONE I KNOW

Someone I know is dying
living the days one by one by one
while the body plans its flight
beyond the antiseptic hallway
and someone else I know—and love—
has fallen in love, has found the one
who makes her want to be herself
on earth all day long

and still crows hurry at dusk
to roosts where young hatch out
to squawk at mothers' bills
until they fly and forget
they are bonded to the ground
by trees, though above us

How we manage
the dying and the loving
our hearts big steamy
sites believers come to
point at, photograph
because here they say a human
did his work each morning
though dying was coming too

Did he walk along the shore and think
the hundred thousand thoughts
everyone collects in a day?
Did he find a separate self
tugged by those loved and leaving?
Does he see, still, the stones
he flung into waves
sinking below their circles?

POEM AGAINST THE RETURNING ANGEL

From my shoulders down to my hips
what am I?—the day I was made
every cell borrowed
from parents what they got
from God—and each cluster
will be recalled
when the bestower returns, sent across time
for gut, glands or lungs
—Heart will not protest much
when it feels him fingering
and my liver will shine
with unearthly light once
plopped in unstainable bowls—

but my arms can fend off
his advent—I can run
and kick, strike at him
who comes to collect mid-section
freight previously signed for
—watch me hurl stones
upward into his descending, soundless
plumes—let him underestimate
nails of my hands
bones of my fingers—
right heel can break an
intended embrace—
I can determine to fight

or love: look up
close the eye
unsure mouth and, last of all
seashell curves of the ear

HAY DAY CANTICLE

after Louis MacNeice's *Autumn Sequel*

The hay was mint and green and grew far off
where our racks went wobbling, each one
pulled by a pair of nags who stopped to cough

now and then a green slobbery spasm the sun
made glimmer so we never thought to bring
a vet's help where age had entered and begun

under that wide blue sky speckled with wings
of hawk and insect and crow, and clouds
coming and going as if pulled on a string

by the wind's long arm, some days crowds
of grey up there huddled together to make
us turn our sweaty collars up, almost proud

we could pitch and work without a break
in any weather, throwing up the cut grass
into the rack, not minding how the snake

flung himself away from our feet—alas
the dogs were on him, flinging his narrow
soul up to those very clouds that passed

without bothering to note among the yarrow
the blood, among the shiny tines of our forks
the abandoned nest of the field sparrow

with its intricate beak-woven fancywork
that made me pause, not to admire but recall
end of day meant school's irksome homework

2.

The day came when the horses were sold
and we gathered in the hay with machines
rectangular bales smelling a little of mould

where they had sat on the cold earth, a screen
for coyotes sneaking toward unaware grouse
and, little more than a child, a young thirteen

I cared a little about who lived, whose spouse
had to be cared for overmuch, a constant
worry and weight so the entire house

was focused on dying, or on some thin aunt
too poor to afford good help, her nieces
coming every day to tend her, her plants

while, thankful for my masculine releases
I lifted the seventy-pound bales aboard
the rack, leapt to the tractor, its tin caprices

easier to learn than the horses'—lord
how I loved those days, sweating freely
under the geese-filled sky, I felt restored

the more tired I became, starting (really)
to understand how I might avoid death
if I worked and kept my mind (ideally)

far from some future's crooked path
that would lead me to women's woes
and never let me catch my breath

3.

Later it was other than I first thought:
the girl, to begin, seemed to think I knew
how to counter the boy in me distraught

by inexpert fumbling, my trembling debut
of manliness there in the mown field
my car lights illuminating the taboo

we'd fallen into after I'd proudly wheeled
off the main road and bumped across
the verge, eager for all to be revealed

at last, her soft spots and my rough sauce
made by some design to meet, everyone said
it was time for each of us to get across

into adulthood though what sudden dread
rose up between us as we kissed and knelt
in that summer-shiver night, the hay spread

beneath our thighs, our moans, my belt
loosed, her dress up-tucked, we already
feeling more than we thought could be felt

by children of our parents, those steady
pale crossed-over ones no doubt asleep
while their bed-made offspring, shocked already

by the too-soon done, became ourselves: she to weep
a little while I gasped and imagined how much higher
my spasm would make next year's hay leap

4.

I wasn't always boorish, I learned a bit, finished
school, got a job here and there, ended up at last
an agricultural feed-supply salesman, undiminished

by my lack of panache—because once again grass
called out to me: "Play ball!" and I became the best
third baseman in our league—loud mouthed with sass—

they'd ever seen, the old men said so, impressed
with my hitting and running, my sliding in to score
they made me see I could afford a puffed-up chest

but what I loved most was the guys and our rapport
and my own small joy kicking up the stubble
that smell of summer dust was like a trapdoor

opening inside me, where I lived my double
life and knew myself—though perhaps not quite well
enough not to get a girl (not that first one) in trouble

and now I drive from town to town, trying not to dwell
on selling to stores and farms the bags, pellets and such
that end up shit, returning to a woman—no belle—

heavyset and perfumed and still trying too much
to be young again when even I have stopped wandering
with my eye among the girls, my fantasy to touch

one who'll bring alive some true sweet pondering
that might explain what went wrong, how I ended up
with a fool's life full of sadness and squandering

5.

Ah, it wasn't always a mess, this life of mine:
I laughed and drank and travelled across borders
into other provinces, landscapes from another time

beyond, entering those mountains, what disorder
in the earth, it seemed to me, rows on white rows
of cliffs and each one holding back its boulders

till I drove through—oh, yes, cars I loved I suppose
more than people because they took me elsewhere
I could pull into an empty hay field and doze

and not have to put out energy, to try to care
so mostly I was happy with myself and in my mind
which I knew wasn't much but at least I was aware

I was no intellect putting on the airs, overly refined
and gassy, or holding forth about local politics
I knew how to talk—a salesman needs to love mankind

a little or at least in the moment, even the dicks
who tried to cheat me or thought I was slow
and wouldn't catch on fast enough to their tricks

though once I made the sale and left their show
behind, what did it matter, soon enough I was free
on the highway again, radio, wind, sometimes snow

the elements my friends not asking much of me
though motels with their thin towels and small soaps
tested me each time, ate up what once was gutsy

6.

Once I almost felt I understood enough to say
something about God—when my boy died
not yet a being and my wife began to pray

those long hours on her knees until she decided
heaven was all false, and she started drinking
silently, then openly, at the pub, and then she lied

and said she hadn't slept with Jim, thinking
I didn't know their affair was front-page news
and the old men turning away, smiling, winking

Jim left her of course, as I knew he would, booze
more his friend than she, and she came back
and tried to make amends—how could I refuse

when I knew her heart was done in, black
with self-regret, filled with pain and shame
as was my own, we made a merry pair, on track

no doubt for some great fight that never came
living our separate lives from then on, amenable
even caring, childless, future-flat, no flame

but there were nights at least we set the table
shared the day's events, came to love, almost
or touched when we washed up, lived a fable

of wrongs forgiven if not forgot, ghosts
that stepped between us when we turned
to one another, then turned back, away, morose

7.

Yes, I told myself, sing, sing, the way my father
sang working with his crops, his fields, his tools
his cap pushed back, as if nothing could bother

his pleasure in feeling his muscles, only fools
would find an indoor life—he often said, smiling—
where each man had to obey someone else's rules

how he would've laughed at me, my constant dialling
up clients and talking sweet, describing the new
best thing I was pushing, my end-of-week filing

because paper he never trusted, found it untrue
too often the way words could be bent or twisted
except for lyrics of the old songs, those with a blues

edge that he made light, he always resisted
that descent into sadness I seemed to make my own
becoming worried, heartless, despairing unassisted

by events—though plenty enough—I was all moan
which is why I think back to him again, his songs
and ease with *things* that baffled and made me groan

and I resolve to find a tune to sing all day long
forcing up a hum until it takes its rightful place
and gladdens my heart and lasts the day, belongs

and replaces all my melancholy, nulls, erases
scenes I can't forget, mistakes made and made again
until at last I am a singing man, full of grace

8.

A travelling salesman is not without his flings
the sweet blond waitress who gave free pie
who would have thought she'd take off her rings

before she crawled into my bed, there to apply
her charms to my tired back at first and then
working her way around to my belly and thigh

getting closer, then stopping and starting again
the way she gave herself so easily, enjoying
me, her lummox, she said, best among men

and how did we know we'd end up destroying
our connection if one of us said too much
about love or the future or some other cloying

kind of talk—Maggie was mine to clutch
but not to hold and she had no thought either
of wanting more from me than a monthly touch

happiness the day I passed through, a breather
from the dullness of her husband's familiar skin
she said, claiming she liked that I was neither

dank nor dry—her words—but good as sin
best of all because transgression gave delight
and made her blush, and all without chagrin

or perhaps just a little guilt, a tiny blight
that came up after we reclaimed ourselves
often wishing we could arrange the entire night

9.

One day driving on a side road I stopped
walked into a field, stood still under the sun
smelled the grass and dust, then dropped

down to my knees, rolled over, stretched one
hand up to block the hot glare and started
thinking: what's my heyday, my home run

to remember forever, but I grew fainthearted
trying to discern if I was actually worth
what the Creator had made before he departed

never again bothering to come down to earth
and tell me, me of all people, that yes
of course there's a reason for your birth

I heard the woodpecker just then bless
the wood he was knocking, though the worm
I wondered what he thought as deathly progress

made its way toward his treetop long-term
home—and I also heard an old crow calling
and his ardent cry reaching me affirmed

I had been spotted, lying there, sprawling
half my mind loose, but some part caught
and just as sudden as sun I started bawling

a child, glad no one saw I was overwrought
touched by those bird songs, by their life
that untied in me an old blood knot

TRAIN RIDE

passing through Linz I notice trains
preternaturally, not the cylinders
for carrying acid chemicals
graffiti on their bulging sides
but older blocky types
of faded wood now silenced
on a weedy siding, while I sit in the upper
section, aware of speed and efficiency

across from me two young men gaze
into a camera steadied by the über-clean
hands of the blond one, occasionally
speaking quiet German phrases
while the old man cross-aisle snorts
as he sleeps though his jaw remains firm
and never once does his mouth fall slack
to reveal a vacuity no one has to see
while I see how I've travelled beyond
the two paragons but haven't yet arrived
at the one who catches his escaping breath
though I also note he's mastered not
sliding on his seat into a heap of age

I turn away from humans close at hand
to look again at boxcars and wonder
what they are filled with, carried
and left behind: routine stuff of light
bulbs and oddments from elsewhere
tractor parts and toiletries, nothing worse
can be imagined today as our train passes
through Linz, bearing me, grateful for
considerate and sleeping companions, easy
to say now we're going somewhere safe

ON THE OCCASION OF VISITING AUDEN'S GRAVE

somehow I don't expect sighing evergreens
or cruel April's birds tuning up their notes
or the autobahn's whine beyond the church's
sweet-cream-pastry-coloured plaster walls
though I recognize the iron cross and plaque
labelling the deceased as poet and man of letters
and somehow the ivy's dense entanglement
surprises me as do wilting winter pansies
on top of the small rectangle of the plot itself
(how can it hold such long, grand bones?)
and a two-pence copper coin lying atop moss
that says he is loved by someone from home
and those admirers from other lands (like me)
know better than to swipe this little token
even as I feel its melancholic foreignness
enter my thumb and vibrate with an eagerness
to claim the wrinkled poet as my own

yes, I know how men slide daily under earth
and what remains of them upside stays briefly
before it too leaves like wind or highway noise
while calamity clots nearby, one hamlet away
even as that woman in her red coat crosses
a green field, happy black terrier leaping up
to her hand, as a crow settles his wings on pale
winter stubble, and an old man in a crushed hat
posts a letter at a yellow box—and may a reply
come sooner than he expects from a grandson
he loves to praise as only a free man can praise

but likely it's a bill, what must be paid
in a certain period before penalties apply
and debts accrue and demands mount
and a day passes in which he fails to relish
this heaven-side of grass, neglects the glory
in birdsong!—and in men whose songs rise
so smoothly from their natures we forget
how both ease and fine form came to pass
out of a morning's work in the low house
with green decorative siding not far from
his grave, a domicile easy to pass by without
a murmur of wonder—though the German words
under his photo leave me squinting, envious
of those who know more than I, who knew him
as a neighbour, summer visitor to Kirchstetten
on a back road bordered by willows ready to bud
from soggy forest floor with leaves faint for now

DISLOCATION

the child takes the hand of an older brother
leads him into a house where a kind-faced
violinist reaches his instrument down
and before the two boys begin
to sing to his vibrato, the child
turns back to remaining
family members clustered outside
tells them to ready their hankies
so sweet will be the music made
for the father, for whom especially
these songs are sung
                    my own damp
pillow awakens me in a foreign bed
where I wonder if this dream
arrives only in dislocation, to uncover
how a constancy remains
and requires thought
so that, here, closer to the village
of my forefathers, its dust
might enter me
                  on this table
peonies eager to open and bless me
with their cut dying—they might have
in incarnations of earlier seeds
graced a meal when my father's father
came home weary
found his family singing not hymns
but rhyming paeans even the youngest
knew were both his own and everyone's

LOVEMAKING IN VIENNA

August night so heavy with damp
all exhaled breaths from the dead
in the Danube are falling upon the city
soggy and hot, and I throw open
casements and hope the famous *Föhn*
with its hint of pinewoods will find me
but it does not, I am too hemmed in:
tall stucco walls, windows overlooking a small
courtyard full of green feathery treetops
climbing up in moonlight—and so later
a woman's moaning slides across the leaves
close by, uninterrupted queen of the night
and I'm waking and not waking but awake enough
to wonder out of which window does love fly

and later still, when silence returns, I'm fully
attentive to hearing it, no traffic beyond my bed
to deflect or ignore
           —and then we're all
drowsy beyond sad dreams, spines feeling
rare breeze so welcome on wet flesh
that wakefulness grows almost into desire
though sleep is strong and best

ALBRECHT DÜRER AND ME

at the Albertina Museum

his entire life he thought
of death approaching
it was the century syphilis arrived
1500 meant the end of time
one self-portrait an imitation
of Christ

for me, it's his rabbit
each ear bent differently, every
whisker visible
its mood pensive
another sort of portrait

and his monogram—
AD, 1502 (same year
his medieval father died)—
floats beneath the brown foot
as I float

back to rodents I snared
in a winter garden
frozen next day
and still the fur soft
(or back to fuzzy lucky
charms on key rings
among coins in pockets
of the slightly odd)

from him almost all
German art springs, begins
from me up pops this poem
when here I stand
(wanting to touch the painting
and feel the fur again)
one of many awed viewers
this young hare has seen
in five centuries
even as he draws into
the calm before trembling
to ponder his animal thought

and from my departing train
I see him once more
a tall buck alert in rows
of early corn, escaped, free of
any frame—though red dots
of waving wild poppies
defining the farmer's field
draw my eye to his readiness
for leaping

SELF-PORTRAIT NUDE

I stand in front of a tortured portrait
completed in 1910 by Egon Schiele:
skin reddish and raw, a scraped skeletal self
tilting, electrified by jagged outline of light
eyes closed, hair livid red blue
elsewhere in this museum
hang works of his other distortions
in legs and torso, some kink of the inner
made visible, along with the more famous
Gustav Klimts though they
failed to hold me as did these hysterical shapes
which perhaps foreshadow the artist's death by
Spanish flu, 1918, thousands dying contorted

and now I recall my father also suffered that
influenza in Detroit where he went to work
in car factories, he and his brother for days
sick in their room, young men—and
did he know they might be dying, waiting
and praying, no doubt they were praying, and
though he believed in the strength of that power
he could not deny the virus, illness eating
in him so he coughed himself up—and still
he did survive, crept out of that stinking house
an emaciated, gaunt adolescent, made
his way back to Canada to live and eventually
make me
                 and I think now some spirit of Egon flew
from Vienna, drawn to my weakened father
who in his fatigue raised an arm above
his burning forehead and deflected it, returning
to himself as he was before he descended
into days of half breathing, half living with death

—and yet part of the painter entered Father
as an unseen arrow that pierced through
matter and was itself released in his last
offspring, so here I stand in this Viennese vault
recognizing myself in these twisting limbs

and later buying a black T-shirt with one of his
signature figures of skewed appendages stencilled
in shiny blue, I almost wish I hadn't succumbed
to such tourist delirium, but I needed an emblem
to remember my long-gone juvenescent wild skin
and jutting bones, my imprisoning self-pity

to evoke him, to keep him close, talisman
to protect me from my own age's plagues
coming from outside on the wind and those
eventualities from within rising up in blood
and phlegm, ushered along by semen and soul

IN HALLSTATT

red hair of the guide leads us down
into earth mined for twenty-seven centuries
though only we and our recent progenitors
are tourists, all earlier visitants came
for salt, their individual stories lost or
merged with legends from the Celt
cemetery exhumed nearby in this valley
shadowed by peaks beyond peaks and
steep walls where nothing clings but myth

had I once been one of those who wore
gold bracelets on his biceps, and if one
such prince would touch me now, will I
know, the shiver of eternal recognition
shocking me backwards out of these
protective overalls all visitors must wear
a gaggle of us turning into a platoon
in red outfits, same for me as for
the Japanese and South Africans

will I walk into these depths older than
possible to grasp, even with the dark
illuminated by the guide's torch and words
and not return to reasoning as a city-walking,
siren-cringing, magic-missing
modern but find beneath these mass clothes
bronze body armour, and in my hand the
amber-embellished hilt of an iron sword
that led me over more than mountains

later we eat fish from the crystal lake
and under the calm of local wine speak of
the last war here, of a mother who carried
to her grave hope her missing son might
yet return, and then I sleep, my femurs not
unlike those in the close-by charnel house
until its flanking church's pre-dawn bells
announce I must begin again the work
of unearthing who I might yet become

A MOMENT OF MISSING BELLS

on a construction site, a crowbar falls on a pail
at such an angle that metal on metal rings out
to the plaza where I sit near mumbling fountains
half in shadow, half in sun, in view of distant water
and I twist my head to catch the sound again

as if a bell *has* rung, and in that instant I walk again
in Wien amidst the pealing, air-filling, calling chimes
resounding out from corner churches, sending their
iron-made messages of attention and intent
through pedestrians hurrying to destinations of

torte trysts, formal assignations or sitting alone
with tiny porcelain cups in hand, which tremble
in sympathetic vibration, and so the big and
little are joined as the hourly resonance
floats over the city, causes its denizens to

gaze upward at spires and to imagine themselves
ascending, asking how it feels to have ascension
inside them, a tintinnabulation growing, climbing out
of one's chest since first burst of the clapper striking
told how a small tick has been carved out of time

LILACS

if only the distance between desires
and me were wider than the walkway's
invitation to stroll among new lilacs
the short time they live with us, soon
rust brown, fragrant only days—
and so pervasive, persuasive the wanting
that overtakes me as I sling my body
along, inviting me to reconceive of
various places it might belong

midway in their transient time
lilacs tease with scent, remind me
I am an earth-thing: fully here
even when travelling toward not-to-be
with edges and urges best left
on beaches, where salt and wind
draw from my skin its remembering
and failures to grasp what comes
when guts will shrivel and
cease—yet I might also
jump to counter-scenes that
revive: how to live with that woman . . .
live like that man . . . laugh like
their child, leap like her dog . . .

THE BRIDGE FROM DAY TO NIGHT

driving back on the Second Narrows
I see the mountains of North Van
rise higher than I imagine
they can, they keep going
up and up, and from the apex
of the bridge with traffic flying
I look directly into
their deepest clefts:
a bear drifts on the trails
and a hiker half falls down
the slope, one arm out
for a sapling to swing around

it's home (box in a box)
that will save me (if not him)
yet I sometimes can't decide
should I go up the Cut
or turn on Main, the only options
I see right now, though late at night
when I give up the day
I dream the bear comes calling

. . . volubly, pointing out below
the valley of small lakes gleaming up
where we're ledge-perched, the wind
inside our jackets, pulling our pockets
before he begins down the trail
into the bottomland, the shining lakes
waiting, to plant some new seed
of blue mirror sheen inside himself
we stop, he talks, and the stream of air
takes the words—

how the timbre of his voice
finds us equals today
and he can scrutinize terrain
as if I were his hunting partner
who knows the paths of animals
their spoor and signs few can read

but I've worn the wrong clothes
from the wrong era and cannot descend
into the valley of the many lakes
their fertile mud, the ducks
and deer, the tang of new willows

I take shelter by a leafless tree
he'll return to tell me
of his last steps into the moist
perpetual spring and summer
lean toward me and shout
against the gale force here, his mouth
near my ear, my head bent to hear him
glad to draw this close
to smell not his old-man
scent but the lily pollen
apple blossom, tiniest hint
of earth set to yield

WALDERSEE CHURCH

I was a boy who sought and found
an oriole shadow falling from wind
past poplars onto our high house wall
and hearing his song, I leapt from
where I was lolling on the grass as
his sound swept along and kept me sweet

till an old woman died, a grandmother
last seen lying abed, air immovable
around her, sons back by the door
my own mother pale with grief
that her mother never did receive
the one flowered dress she desired
which my grandfather would not buy
his tight-fisted fear of not having dollars
deep inside the pockets he soon took
earthward, his stick left behind

and with that I had crossed a demarcation
understood death meant my mother's
dying, and I knew how I would fail
if she were not available for my ease
each day, and so I sat in that church
and wailed even louder than she
because I did not know of her relief
that the old woman had slipped past pain
uplifted somehow above the altar and
statue of Jesus, also immovable
in red robes, starred palms out

I brought from that forming hour a
precise smell of foliage: funeral wreaths
bore an acid scent (as if decay had
begun—and it had begun, I had to admit
its idea rooted in me did not die), whiff
I catch walking on November leaves
roused by a sun-borne breeze

SLEEPWALKING

I arose from my bed
walked out of my room, a boy
who found his way to the kitchen
pulled back a wooden chair
to climb on the table
where the previous evening
he'd sat with his family eating
pancakes, which perfected
in him the trick of walking
while asleep, softly
stepping past logic toward
the edge of the oilcloth
worn white from use and wiping

his mother standing below him now
arms upraised, hair dishevelled from
night, her face wearing that
old worry, always what if
she hadn't been there, and future
fears, for what of cars and
girls and finding somewhere
safer than this nighttime ledge

and the boy came awake to the thought
of the horses capable of standing
while sleeping, huge nodding heads
not bearing them to the ground—
he'd seen them lying flat
though rarely, and once one
stretched out and never did rise
to shudder off dust—
and day awareness came to him
in his desire to keep wakeful
somehow, even if his mother's arms

were welcome, and he did not mind
when she carried him back
to his still-warm bed, that space
sometimes like the one I inhabit now
in my daily to and fro
and out of which I wonder
when I might awaken

THE PHOTOGRAPHER

. . . at the edge of this group of alert men
—all men—in the concentration camp, all
wearing ties because it's Christmas Eve
(so says a propped sign with Gothic letters)
German emigrants collected
by the *War Measures Act* in 1915
O, Canada! you do not know
the silences you have bequeathed unto
generations because no man here could breathe
knowing the outgoing air would shatter
all beliefs with the violence of its yell

sitting two men away from my grandfather
at the end of the row where he's just
nipped in, the photographer is pert, peering
into his own camera set up to take in
these lines of prisoners, their tinsel tree
the bent mattresses in the bleachers
of the fairgrounds where they sleep
some leaving behind a corpse
swinging, which internees see first
come morning and cold and gruel from
other-accented guards with Ross rifles
and long-reaching bayonets

my grandfather sits here, shocked rigid
what of his wife on her own, on the hard farm
and with children? I see his panic
the mark of betrayal on his face
that he was invited (like many)
to occupy the West, that he left
his ancestral home not knowing
the drift of history would ensnarl him
and, today, he's determined to show
that whatever the camera captures
it is not humiliation swelling within

LARGE, BROWN GELDING

. . . serves by pulling and stopping, then
pulling again, hard, side by side with
the black mare, head down, braced to haul
a load of stones—I remember mostly stones
and hot hairy rumps, hiss of their tails
against cruel flies, large liquid eyes
a child dives into and imagines himself
some other being, greater than mere boy
until one day the gelding's replaced: a mule
grey-wizened in harness, glory-lacking
but not dead—I rail at my mother: why
was I not told, why did I not deserve
to know? she says little, says my father
will have the answer—and so he enters
our presence striding, cracked leather boots
and cracked leather face like that of
a Balkan partisan who fights in winter
and has no patience for chatting
about natural dying that any worthy son
would absorb or toss behind him
he says "appointments" and explains
no further, lets words fade, shorthand
he expects me to grasp, and I see now
he is old, as I am also old and must save
my rage for matters other than death
and in what is not said I hear where next
I must learn to live—and before I turn
to own my adult ache, I think of the gelding
wanting no more than his burden
of inevitability, and I promise to hold to
the memory of his strength, his last
groan of power spent departing, leaning

under a heavy sun, the very one
making my father fret, his worn boots
scuffing dirt, raising a snowy dust

ON OUR WALK ALONG THE DANUBE

the summer evening offers
a sunset with dark colours
and two kinds of time:
                                    first, the river
sends its weight against shore
and bridge and without malice
intends to be in Budapest by morning
yet remain here in its molten
manner, its trick of staying and leaving

then, above us the castle is unmoved:
its stone knows centuries can be
square, each tower a testament to
history's way, which is stop-and-go
only the flag at its highest turret
allowed to change its design
and colours as monarchs deign

and perhaps a third time exists
in we who walk the narrow path
sometimes of packed sand
so I think we may be stepping
outside the stony past and beyond
the flowing future, and our faces
soften in their tenderness for the light
settling on us a glow, the reflection
off water when we know we can linger

but now Susan pulls from her bag a sweater
the night air a new reminder, and we hurry
onto the bridge whose steel flanks
we press our hands against, feeling the sun
captured there and still radiating heat
though it has already gone from us

I LOOK DOWN INTO MY BACK LANE

mostly men without packages
not shopping, not on errands
they stop in a parking spot
cupping a hand against gusts
to light a smoke, stooped, they step
forward again, not with determination
not rambling either, the lane
not green or open or calm enough to warrant
pause or strolling—in caps and anoraks
legs thin and wide apart, so I can picture
skinny bodies under bulky sweaters,
and some unshaven ones can't remember
how to straighten their bones

would they like a word?
but what could I say? that if you look at
what keeps you unfree, that thing
most hard to look at
even if you can see it at all
much less name it, if, if . . .

each man loyal to his own word
it might be defiance or dependence
difficult to deal with
though walking helps mightily

I could say, hey
you, down there, look up! (they never do)
it's not just me you'll see
yes, concrete balconies crowded
with flowering pots and higher still
the crows and gulls wheeling, and in time
if weather is willing, the unclouded moon
and her stars

ON THE DUAL NATURE OF THINGS, I WRITE

that a solitary gull floats between high-rises
with aplomb and grace, gliding past
balconies far above my own
his immaculate white, airy curves
I may describe as angelic
that apparition-like way of arriving
then vanishing behind a tower
(saving his squawk for fellow gulls
or flapping, enraged crows)

yes, I know of his appetite and table manners
his strutting entitlement as he approaches
a burst garbage bag, his fury
when any other creature comes near
the blows his wings can deliver, the depth
his beak can sink into the soft stuff of the dead
his eagerness to eat what's vile
and leaking and staining asphalt
with a smear only winter rains will erase

but today he owns the air, he is beautifully
there, to remind me that his sea is near
and a joy to remember especially when
I recall my inland time in cities devoid of
sea-cries that prompt me here
to lift my eyes and watch his swift tilting
as he adjusts his trajectory to the flow
of wind blowing in from the west
from the ocean, which he helps me
celebrate: he says if I follow his flight
I will find that salty, sandy, flexible edge
along which I might stride, or stumble
if I am not aware of the flashing wave tips
offering their news of light to bird and man

THE SKINNY MAN WITH THE STIFF LEG

kicks at a piece of trash
a white circle that once covered
takeout Thai food, and his good foot
is strong, the paper flies a little, achieves
lift-off before it settles to the edge
of the lane, marginalized

like the man himself, and I wonder
has he always taken a path where
he can walk and watch, directing
his discontent at rubbish—was it that
he loved and wanted love
that was not returned?

I've seen him standing where others
are hurrying, his baseball cap
down to hide his eyes
though his reddish hair sticks out

his freckled arms, his dusty pants
of the kind not seen anymore in stores
the lack of colour in his shirt
all tell me he is poor, that he wanders
the back street to keep himself company
to forget who might have propelled him
into some other way of being

he reminds us as we pass by
of our own faltering, as recent
as this morning when we thought of
someone who still matters
words, voice, text silent now
and the place we occupy
unfinished within ourselves

pushing forward, so we find
our centres lodged in other people
who have no knowledge
of our state, themselves busy with
moments of kicking garbage

HE ENTERS THE LANE LUNGING

as so many men lunge, his torso
tipped forward out of faded jeans
glasses blanking the world
so he sees only that step after step
won't allow inside emptiness
to suffice, to slow him
not into torpor but peace, peace
at least, at last, enough
so he can stop striding

his grey hair uncut in a while
arms swinging, but he's not noticeably
mad unless many are crazed this way
by the overflowing that drives us
into anonymous laneways
where we turn our faces away
to feel free from the scrutiny
and then disregard of others
—free of fleet entanglements—
no one to sidestep except one's self
which can't be done, there's no leaving
him behind, his hold reinforced
by every tread on this prowl

then the man is gone, out the end
of the lane—and has he felt the sunshine
that surely pulled him with its promise
from his rooms, and how is he now
when he turns the key and re-enters
the familiar where earlier he felt
stirring, then flooding, that urge
to plunge beyond silence?
how able to stand still instead
on the tiny atoll of mere continuance?

AT NIGHT DARKNESS FILLS THE LANE

with a solidity unknown by day:
black flows in and obliterates
landmarks—what exists at noon
when seen by moonlight
glows inaccurately
all angles sinister

a rat races across the expanse
its eye providing a single spark
its claws on concrete a clatter so soft
it can only be heard in the hours
after midnight or after two on weekends
when residents succumb at last to sleep

occasionally a bulb burns above
this zone of collected obsidian and
stays alight throughout the night
to hold off fears, as if a face can fall
into its dreamtime shape more agreeably
while still illuminated, not loosening
as it might when dark steals from it
the strength of features known
at noon, what we know of one another

and wish to know, not wanting
that other creature whose slack jowls
and lips wet with drool turn us away
so we find ourselves looking out again
into the night and seeing in
windows the reflections we must
look beyond even if fearful that
what lies in the lane at this hour
cannot be good for us, the half
shapes that just a few hours ago
were bushes, poles and posts
with no malign intent

AT END OF DAY A MOMENT

comes when rays of setting sun
extend their promise out of
the sky and provide to earth
filmic beams, reminding us
biblical times are here, too
even if a holy hour lasts visually
only one minute as light strikes
up through clouds into space
we believe was made for us

but here in the lane we cannot see
this brief beauty: our apartments
block the way west, and yet
we gain in what is reflected above
on high windows: a surging
glow deepens and presents orange
rectangles behind which we know
families gather for meals, some
squabbling, pulling down blinds
not wanting the blinding final
glare gifted to them in the turning
from one time of day to another

older loners look and ponder
who they are to have arrived here
in this fading, the clouds a painting
of a master colourist in gold and grey
and cream and beige and a blue that dims
its cerulean in honour of coming night
to become as transparent as a page
I might write upon had I a stylus
of lightning or a wand built from
the brightness of an evening star

HOW MANY OF US REMAIN UNFINISHED

I wonder when I look down to the lane
and see someone I cannot fully see
half-hidden under his umbrella
wind occasionally lifts to reveal
moustache and frown, swarthy
sunken cheeks so perhaps a foreigner—
aren't we all? as we lean against
rain and without saying as much
ask how do we access the good god
part of ourselves that often arrives
only as a curse, not what we crave
although what that man below wants
I cannot know—only the highly attuned
among us can pick up all frequencies—
I sense nothing at this distance
except haste in the way he shifts
the umbrella to his left hand
without a glove, a black umbrella
but even so how easy to picture
part of him collapsing when the one
he wants does not want him, a state
that completes incompleteness and that
he works at denying, knowing eventually
all desire dims like a shoreline
when the ship sails, and on its deck
he tastes salt wind alone

SOME DAYS I HEAR THOUGHTS

from those walking below
*how I want just one more juicy meeting
of merry limbs* and the dog on the leash
held by the woman a bit bowed by
years of desire turns to his mistress
surprised by a new perfumy vibration
then returns to messages left in grass

if only I had tried a little harder back then
comes floating up often in the afternoon
wafting by in a dark balloon, almost black
air seeping out of its wrinkled self
impossible to continue up to heaven for
those answers, sinking back to the thinker

I like it here but it's not like home
in this city of immigrants, skin tone
and body shape common, comfortable
still the yearning carries on, causes
feet to drag, the overheavy briefcase
no substitute for lively, dancing nights

and it's true, the clarity of
our last incarnation will be as birds
causes the gulls to scream and
the crows to somersault down from
perches, starlings to chatter
their secret has been revealed

HERE COMES A FACE MADE UGLY

by male anger, the twist of mouth
barely holding back curses
and the muttering ready to blow
as his lips protrude, ears glow red
eyes hooded yet unable to contain
the hurt self, and these combine
to frighten one who might bring
solace, if there even were anyone
whose presence softened his visage
and what could I do to draw him
from the bile that rises, and recalling
what works for me, I yell down
"Look up and let it rain in your eye"

but he does not hear, he's stepped
so deeply alone into himself that
he cannot be reached, and I hesitate
to fling anything else his way—surely
if words fail, my rose petals would
drift past unnoticed, my small
poems shaped into paper darts
would strike against his cap, a further
irritant against which he would rage
to be so bothered by the world when
all he wants is to be free from it

whereas today I love all I survey
with such surety that I may step
from this perch—the air half supports
my falling self, and as I speed toward
this maddened one, he will blurt out
in astonishment all that plagues him
so my landing, hard as it is, makes
him fumble with his phone
and shock softens, reverses
what a moment ago he loathed

A BODY FALLS OUT OF THE SKY, LEGS UP

the heavy head dropping first, this
I fear from the towers that rise
above the lane where I watch
unidentifiable . . . women? men? seldom
children? scurrying on high balconies
press against railings, lean far out
not suspecting the sudden give
of rain-soddened support until
someone tumbles, arcs, grasping air

I stand rooted on my ledge, shooing
pigeons away, tend to geraniums
scissors in hand, snipping deadheads
always aware of the edge as close
as choice itself, though certain annihilation
might turn into broken only, unable and
immobile and a brain babbling
that the angel one hoped for did not
materialize, instead now shrill voices
of should have and never ever, never ever
and never ever again on the ward
all windows closed against any
fluttering beyond the pane

OF COURSE THE GODS HAVE FLED THE LANE

filled it with film trucks, attendants
while I want skylarks to ascend
and remind me I have a destiny
waiting, if not here then beyond
men and women bedecked
with tools at their waists, phones
in their hands, duct tape dangling
all creating light and shadow
to entertain us when we get glum
because we're ordinary after all

yet ordinary is so vast it's enough
or should be even if not complete
that god part missing, replaced
even if irreplaceable—still, we're
good at adapting to lesser forms

that the crow that lurks at the edge
of this stuck cavalcade doesn't sing
as sweetly as the storied lark
doesn't limit his intelligence, and so
I urge my thinking to accept
the day as is and what it offers me
which might not be the highest light
but still the sun lands on the dark bird
and makes it shine

"FUNNY"

Miro points to a row of second-floor windows
(on some *ulica* / street whose name escapes)
each ornate in history's way, and tells me
he spent years in those bright rooms
singing in a choir, "a funny time," he says
and several steps later as we cross
tram tracks, I ask, "funny how?"
in Canada we might mean
those days were somehow oddly *off*
but he explains, "a time without problems"
and I understand, "a time of fun"

even small differences continue to surprise
and reveal who each of us is, what
our cultures and languages have made
like his number 1 with its slight
tilt with an added angle at the top
that risks becoming a seven, as if
haunted by a touch of the Cyrillic

and he has little use for "I" because
when admiring a house, for example
his grammar leads him to say "it likes me"
and so his world is animated, filled
with metaphor cheerfully directing
·its attention onto him, greeting him daily
while his Canuck friend must search
in himself, object after object singled out
to find what is enlivened out there
and so misses the rush of feeling from the world
continuously coming to embrace him

PREŠPORÁK

on a street with stones that cause my feet
to twist, with graffiti-fed walls
that lean in as they rise to the gold
and green steeple above Michael's Gate
a one-room café serves coffee from Rwanda
or an elderflower and thyme concoction
that liberates the tongue into summer

surrounded by old books, students
talk *hovädiny*, or so Miro says, trash
I understand nothing they say though
they laugh and carry on, unconstrained
I remember my own carefree
college days when I discovered
poetry could be mine and perhaps
philosophy except Kant's door never did
open the way Dr. Owen claimed it would

the menu's tattered and stained
with charm, fingered, considered and
spilled upon by Slovak coffee-lovers
as they turn toward one another
to whisper little words that grow large
while all the doodads listen in: dusty
typewriter, telescope aimed up,
an unlocked bird cage, a model ship
setting sail by the cake display, windows
open to the narrow street, light falling off
medieval walls, no rhetoric
only time apparently stalled
as if to allow friendships
to stream as easily as daylight in June

even if outside and not far away
apartment blocks of Communist architecture
pile up on one another, concrete on concrete
with little grace and less sunlight, to remind us
that even amid the simple connections
men by casual chat co-create
through caffeine, a shadow may fall
and block one mind from another
so we will require all our thoughts like beams
to break the man-made stoniness and yield
a softer, longer line of beauty

Hero and Leander in Bratislava

the old story is revealed to me via
five tapestries hanging in a palace
seventeenth-century English threads
hidden in the walls, discovered
during renovations, a complete set
creates the outcome of tragic love:
pale, mourning Eros peers
into the water that swept Leander
to his death, as if to find consolation
not reminders, his short bow broken

but what's a god to do when called
as he was called to draw the man
toward Hero, his beloved? whose
many-threaded features shine
with passivity as if she has seen
Eros's failure to calm the elements—
and what is love if not
what's stronger than the ordinary
day with its wind and waves?

faced with the sad end to this myth
and faced with the millions of threads
and decades of work, English
weavers going blind, centuries-old
repairs in the fabric along the edges
how easy to forget that first came love
Leander wild at the water's edge
swimming into forbidden space

ZAJTRA

part of me stays behind
in Bratislava, walks in snow
beside a city lake, no footsteps yet
to shadow the white path
but now, look: a smoking
squat man with a scowl he's been bearing
for some time, brown trousers
pushed into waterproof boots
well worn, their comfort though
does not stop him from glowering
so accustomed to how wet snow
sucks at his soles, but that is not
the source of his sourness—even so
we manage a glance at one other
though how much more I need
to grasp what has turned him
against this snow, which he scuffs,
against the grey light over the lake
after the white summer swans have flown
where he cannot go—oh, he has the euros
but no distances in his heart, what worries him
lies close to home, in his apartment
he hates the dog, maybe, that barks at night
past the hotel and near to Bajkalská
where the heavy traffic runs
the Škodas aimed at a workday
because it is morning, already tomorrow—
zajtra—where anything can still happen
so the part of me that stays behind
starts out again from Ondavská Street
as the snow falls

LAVENDER SACHETS

first in the Dubrovnik market
from a giant whose blue eyes
search and insist
his flowers will last
and I believe he finds
more than a sightseer
seeking a local's blessing
I leave one in my suitcase
one in the cupboard for pillows.

next in Zagreb I see
the hurried crook of a man's
shoulder blades, sun a hot shock
among citizens carrying
transacted vegetables
greens and browns, and red
his ribbon, on one sachet
not tied quite tight so it spills
while a second bundle haunts
a closet, the clothes there
awaiting transport to bags, bins

wizened woman in Bratislava
her smile easeful, her gesture
without grasping, affection
for passersby true, and so I buy
a bundle, go back for another
wanting some of her light
one of hers I sleep with
the other I stash in the sticky
wooden desk drawer
I rarely open—but
overcome its resistance
and I am returned at once

to her gnarled golden hands
coin aglow against deep lifelines
perfumed by purple fields

SMUTNÝ

means "sad" in Slovak, maybe
homesick—everyone knows
how the struck chest sags
how the twist in the valves
yields an arid song

we must turn our faces
away from friends when
such feeling builds, fearing
kindness will trigger
the uprush of tears

when asked, "what gives
strength?" Miro looked away
said, "boyhood returning
before sleep," sweet warmth
he savoured, a nakedness

that gave for one moment
assurance to continue—and if
perturbing events prevailed
to je život—it is life—not
to diminish but to accept

that fullness extracted a price
he paid at evening
in order to arise next morning
reborn, the old *smutný* cloak
not to be worn at all that day

DRIVING COUNTRY ROADS IN SLOVAKIA

father and son up front joke
in language I can't follow
while the radio alternates between Jagger
and Vivaldi, and so we pass harvested fields
and roadside shrines to the suffering
crucified Christ with fresh plastic flowers
then hilltop castle ruins, goldenrod and lupine
ageless in their wild places
though their names here slip off my tongue
and dip away like the swallows
bobbing out of the creeks

then a derelict factory raises
its Communist brick chimney to mark
the passage of time, while Roma men
stand still on the roadside
tilting baskets toward us
mushrooms, blueberries for sale
as we breeze by

and now my driving friend points out
the steel factory celebrating sixty years
of making, and I catch as well
the steeple of a church
its Russian letters advertising
future space in the cemeteries we only
glance at, at the moderate speed
we've adopted for sliding through
one village and then another
satellite dishes aimed west
clouds of busybody flower-faces flowing
off the balconies, geraniums stiff and watchful

MY SLOVAK FRIENDS

invite me on their August drive
from Bratislava twelve hours to the Adriatic
where red, yellow, green towels
drape from balconies (semaphores
of salty pleasures) and old men
blackened by heat and history
crowd wooden benches and scowl
not one with dark glasses, each
facing the glare of a Balkan sun
as if it were nothing more
than an acquaintance

my friends and I deepen our time together
walking a cliff path edged with whitecaps
and aquamarine toward a haven
where small stones press on our feet
and we lie speechless as lizards
skin darkening, until waves invite us in
or light fails and we gather
ourselves up like wet towels
and return through the buzz of cicadas
to our temporary home

later, travelling away from the sea, I learn
at a highway stop with iffy Wi-Fi
that a friend has died, one who once
held me honestly, and I know again
how each loss matters the most, now
as we pass dry pine hills in Croatia
below distant leafless peaks
from which a soul might be launched
into constellations of white abundance
we call clouds .

SPA, PIEŠŤANY

brought here by the kindness of others
I step into the mirror pool
and my limbs grow heavy with heat
mud oozes up
between my toes and I rub it on
chest and arms, an old soft armour
entering my skin

now I am swaddled in warm blankets
and on the swelling music from above
my mother's here to see what I've become—
she smiles to see unwashed mud
on my feet and does not mind that
my body has aged as hers has not, she's
perfect in her forest green sweater
hair dark and wavy, and a jewel
upon her breast shines gold

she touches me, says I have grown
well beyond the romping, running
child, and laughing, she leaves, rising up
and I recall her crooked hands
from the time when she was my age now
how they would have taken in
the earth's heat here—and she floats away
toward the kindness of those awaiting her
out where lime trees wave with ease

Devín Castle

a ruin above the confluence of
the clear Morava with the deeper
darker Danube it fails to influence
and where men watched from heights
while water flowed past and past
endless in the possibilities of seasons
and terrors but also hours when
a guardsman's attention drifted toward
his night meal of meat, nuts or soup
while the wind blew his way,
the smells of mud and freshets spilling
near fresh burial mounds

and as he fingered his iron weapons
one slipped from his animal belt
to appear much later among amber
in an exhibit around which students
cluster, perhaps one of them aware
how time has thrown him up here
among his smoking, joking peers
to speak Slovak, to wear jeans
to find his body a mystery he worries
may never be easily understood

under my hand the cold rock that forms
this wall is solid, but I know better:
Miro takes my photo, which becomes
a *memento mori* when days from now
I discover it has remained unchanged
in my camera—still the same squint
the grey sky behind showing no sign
of Perun, god of lightning and thunder—
whereas this very hand is less

the sure thing, and yet it serves still
to crumble more stone
into the river below as I reach out
to my friend's hand and climb down from
the bastion—and so we return to our own
sensibilities, heartened here among
scrambling teens ablaze, the beauty of
a summer evening before them
sunlight slanting into warm gold
just at that moment when it sinks—
which I might notice more than they

Kamzík

a communications tower that on a clear day
looks into Austria, Hungary, the Czech Republic
from up here I survey Bratislava
breathe such clean air, recall flowers
that tremble in the forest sunshine
and forget about that staring couple
below, how they smoked and scowled
watching me as if I were the attraction
perhaps because I spoke a language
that sounded unmelodic to them, unable
themselves to roll English words just as I
cannot vibrate my tongue in Slovak

and where is the tongue in English
and not in Slovak? questions
that had never occurred to me
though now I hear the clicking and clacking
of consonants as they fall on my slanted ear
and sometimes are not heard at all though
I am a willing student, so today I think
I might speak more easily with the white
flowers on the trail down from the tower
than to that twosome, sepals and petals
might open at my words, as willing to hear
as I am charmed to know them

what a bounty that man and woman
might have shared with me:
we could point to the white flower
and say its name, each in our own
tongue, the way we could laugh
at the strangeness as it leaves our mouths
when we attempt the foreign word
and the smiles that linger even after

we have parted, especially if we have
shaken hands and agreed without words
that our worth is stronger than words

and yet, and yet, to someone who sounds
as we sound, we would happily spill the story
of how we wished the light in the other's eye
had translated into a tumult of meaning
the wet taste of talk that helps us
as daily as bread, human as breath

SLOVAKS WEAR THEIR HISTORY AS A HEAVY COAT

or as a shawl, breezily, or even not at all,
free to disown the bloodshed and errors
made by ancestors—surely unendurable
any other way—and I see the spirit
the young manage here: to stay uncrushed
by the weight of tyrants and betrayers, tanks
in the street, Brezhnev in Bratislava

I see more: these men, women embrace
impending and present freedoms even if
the past has a hand on their shoulder
gripping fingers reminding with
a pressure that never entirely
ceases, and still, still, many act honourably
even with this encumbrance and so
have not been felled

I fly home to my enclave of peace,
and the history that I have swallowed here
slowly begins to go down my throat
though never gone from my table
and when I revisit the tribulation
I felt there, then even more
I picture my friends before I sleep
touch their heads and pray
not to any Unseen but for
their soul force to continue

and as I drift into dream I admit
to my errors of ignorance, so much
I can never know, about the trains
in the night, their cargo looking out
and to my error of arrogance
that among all peoples on earth
I or anyone is free

PERHAPS MY FATHER WAS RIGHT . . .

we never talked about the ins
and outs of living, never went
heart to heart about work
and pain and people, but
I saw my future by the way
his body broadened, that same
thickening our Prussian forebears
displayed even though
as young men their strength
carried them without weight
their culture utterly Protestant
hard-working, honest, loyal

would he have read the books
I find I am reading now? about
refugees fleeing from Russians
1945, he might have been there
sleeping on straw, lice-infested,
extended family to a room, an
elder dying, hasty burial in a bag
under a roadside pine tree
the handcarts picked up and moving
west, skirting Berlin's smoke and ash

but he was born in 1901 Ontario
a calm place on the world map
I knew he was grateful but haunted
nonetheless by a possible past
starving in a Soviet prison camp, not
what he became: my farming father
straight furrows from his plough
the tines of his hayfork shining
whose own immigrant father was
unfairly interned in friendly Manitoba
1915 after which my dad with his
Old World name Alfred Gustav
refused to speak German again
a blood geography I missed
his way of telling me
I'd have plenty enough
to carry without the sounds
his language transmits, though
still I'd like to know how I might
write this poem in his words
that never-forgotten tongue
supplanted by his son's

ACKNOWLEDGEMENTS

The poems presented here were published between 1971–2023.

I had a great deal of help in the selecting. I am grateful for the four friends who read my books: Russell Thornton, gillian harding-russell, Mike Jaeggle, John Fisher. I would also like to thank Lorna McCallum. Their choices and suggestions have been invaluable. I would also like to thank the editors, publishers and readers of the books listed in the table of contents.

PUBLICATIONS

Mindscapes: poems by Paulette Jiles, Susan Musgrave, Tom Wayman, Dale Zieroth, edited by Ann Wall, Anansi 1971:
    The Hunters of the Deer
    Glenella, Manitoba
    1) 120 Miles North of Winnipeg
    2) Detention Camp, Brandon, Manitoba
    Father

Clearing: Poems from a Journey, Anansi 1973:
(includes poems above first published in *Mindscapes*)
    The Mountains Have Not Yet Entered
    Beautiful Woman
    Lake
    Waiting at Evening

Mid-River, Anansi 1981:
    Baptism
    The Truck That Committed Suicide
    Out Walking
    Journey: Going In / Getting Out

When the Stones Fly Up, Anansi 1985:
    When my cows break loose
    1956: The ambition of the eldest son
    1956: The old Lutheran pastor
    When the stones fly up
    Returning to a town
    The field
    The boat
    The birds stay with him
    Born in Europe

The Weight of My Raggedy Skin, Polestar 1991:
    Death of the Violin
    Aphasia
    David Dale
    Here on the Coast

How I Joined Humanity at Last, Harbour 1998:
Father's Work
My Mother's Wail
A Story
How I Joined Humanity at Last
The Exhausted Past
Reasons for Living
The Way Past Words
The Beautiful Voice of the Undertaker
The Man Who Invented the Turn Signal

The Tangled Bed, Reference West 2000:
The Owl
My First Job
Dream

Palominos, Gaspereau Press 2000:
Edge

Crows Do Not Have Retirement, Harbour 2001:
Method
What To Do
Prayer for a Friend
Crows Do Not Have Retirement
The Options

The Village of Sliding Time, Harbour 2006:
How I Came to Be
Had I Stayed on the Farm

Dust in the Brocade, The Alfred Gustav Press 2008:
Japanese Mallow

Berlin Album, Rubicon Press 2009:
Postcard from Italy

watching for life, McGill-Queen's 2022:
>I look down into my back lane
>on the dual nature of things, I write
>the skinny man with the stiff leg
>he enters the lane lunging
>at night darkness fills the lane
>at end of day a moment
>how many of us remain unfinished
>some days I hear thoughts
>here comes a face made ugly
>a body falls out of the sky, legs up
>of course the gods have fled the lane

the trick of staying and leaving, Harbour 2023:
>"funny"
>Prešporák
>Hero and Leander in Bratislava
>zajtra
>lavender sachets
>smutný
>driving country roads in Slovakia
>my Slovak friends
>Spa, Piešťany
>Devín Castle
>Kamzík
>Slovaks wear their history as a heavy coat

unpublished
>perhaps my father was right . . .

ABOUT THE AUTHOR

Photo by Laura Grant

David Zieroth's most recent books of poetry are *the trick of staying and leaving* (2023) and *watching for life* (McGill-Queen's 2022). *The Fly in Autumn* (2009) won the Governor General's Literary Award and was nominated for the Dorothy Livesay Poetry Prize and the Acorn-Plantos Award for People's Poetry in 2010. Zieroth won the Dorothy Livesay Poetry Award for *How I Joined Humanity at Last* (1998). He lives in North Vancouver, BC, where he runs The Alfred Gustav Press and produces handmade poetry chapbooks.